Gen Zero College Debt

azLearning Publishing

Published by azLearning Publishing, 2024.

While every precaution has been taken in the preparation of this book, the publisher assumes no responsibility for errors or omissions, or for damages resulting from the use of the information contained herein.

GEN ZERO COLLEGE DEBT

First edition. October 29, 2024.

Copyright © 2024 azLearning Publishing.

ISBN: 979-8227656940

Written by azLearning Publishing.

Table of Contents

Chapter 01: Straight Up

Gen Z, you don't have to sacrifice your future by drowning in massive college debt. You don't have to follow the outdated path of starting college on someone else's terms. In fact, you don't have to enroll in college at all! Your future is yours to shape—-boldly, freely, and on your own terms.

This is your time, Gen Z! The world is full of opportunities that didn't even exist a few years ago, and you're perfectly positioned to take advantage of them—whether you decide to go to college or not.

This book could not have been written three or more years ago.

Need proof?

Think about recent history. The pandemic, the recent events at college campuses, and the present economic challenges had not yet occurred.

Your future is in your hands and more exciting than ever. Just look at the changes around us. The rise of blockchain technology, the explosion of generative AI, and the evolving job market where more and more companies are hiring based on your skills, not your degrees—this is the landscape you get to navigate. You don't have to be locked into outdated advice about college being the only way to success.

In fact, if you are getting your advice about college planning from pre-pandemic and pre-AI sources, you might want to discount that advice by about 60 or 70%—probably even more. The world has changed! Technology and labor market changes are accelerating.

The continued high cost of a college education has always been on everyone's radar. Check out the graphs. Up and up goes the tuition graph line, year after year, with no end in sight. Tuition prices are up over 188% over the past 24 years. (source: Bureau of Labor Statistics). According to the College Board, tuition at public four-year universities has nearly tripled since 1990 and has outpaced price increases at public two-year and private universities. Families make substantial financial sacrifices, take out loans, and even mortgage their homes. It's easy to feel like you're being pushed into this system without being told the whole story. And Gen Z, you are seeing through it. You're asking the right questions: Is college really worth it?

Yes, tuition is sky-high, but guess what? GEN Z's FRUSTRATION LEVEL OVER ALL OF THIS IS EVEN HIGHER!!! (caps on purpose) What matters is that you have a plan that works for you—one that doesn't saddle you with debt but still helps you chase your dreams.

If you decide to go to college, there are more ingenious ways to do it. We strongly recommend considering community college first. Or get a company like Starbucks to help pay for your tuition while you work. Or you'll decide to jump into the workforce, start your own business, or take a gap year to figure things out. Whatever path you take should be on your terms—not dictated by outdated expectations or the pressure of debt.

The economics behind this skyrocketing tuition is as basic as supply and demand. Colleges are incentivized to increase tuition since the government is underwriting (financing) the whole process with limitless student loans. Follow the money. With guaranteed government loans, reasons to control the cost of education evaporate. The entire educational system encourages high school students to "follow your dreams" on to the major and the college that'll be "your perfect fit." This is all without a realistic cost/benefit assessment, of course.

Gen Z enrollment in colleges is down. They are questioning the sanity of all of this. They know they have been misled (which is a polite way of saying "lied to.") Gen Z is asking if college is worth it, after all.

So much has changed in the world. Especially the educational world. There has been a real clearing out of American academia. And, if you think the world of higher ed has stayed the same, I wonder if you have been paying attention.

Gen Z ... will you change and adapt for your own personal benefit? Or will you hit the snooze button on life's alarm clock?

If you are interested in subjects such as learning, education, your career, utilizing your talents and creativity, making money, and personal freedom, please continue to read.

Gen Z ... the new choices and opportunities you have in front of you are A M A Z I N G !!! The options and opportunities go far beyond career and monetary benefits. It is about personal and financial freedom and independence.

If you have older siblings who are Millennials, they had some of these choices, but they were less evident and plentiful than they are now.

And indeed, your parents did not have these choices.

For the most part, the old world wants you to graduate from high school as best you can and apply and enroll in a college suitable for your pursuits so that you can support the next level of educational bureaucracy in this country. Do your fair share for the academic industrial complex. Topped off with plentiful student loans, of course.

This does not address whether high school adequately prepared you for your next educational challenges in college.

Needed to be addressed, of course, is whether enrolling in college with its bloated educational environment and with the associated bloated education student loan debt that you'd be assuming is the best academic and personal choice for you at this time.

Most importantly, this book is here to help you build a plan that avoids debt. Imagine graduating debt-free, with the freedom to chase whatever drives you—whether starting a career, traveling the world, or continuing your education. That's not just a dream; it's a strategy, and we will show you how to do it.

So, what are these wonderful options that we speak of here?

There are four main options we will be exploring.

We will call them PLAN A, B, C, and D.

> **PLAN A:** attend college (after high school)
>
> **PLAN B:** do not attend college (begin your career)
>
> **PLAN C:** Hybrid solution (delay attending college)
>
> **PLAN D:** The Starbucks solution (get Starbucks or some other corporation to pay for your college)

For example, if you choose PLAN A or PLAN C, you will read how community college is a brilliant, cost-effective decision. Direct entry into the workforce or entrepreneurship are viable options with PLAN B or PLAN D and should not be discouraged.

More options, better options, and more exciting options are one thing. However, if you select one of those options and get your college diploma and graduate DEBT FREE, that would be the best of all worlds. Correct?

That is precisely the purpose of this book. The book is written to encourage you to employ a zero-debt strategy with your college career. It will give you the tools and ideas to put this into action. Follow your dreams, yes. But follow them debt-free.

So, here's to you, Gen Z! You've got this, with or without college. The future is full of opportunities, and you're ready to take them on. Let's get started!

Chapter 02: The Crushing Crisis of Student Debt

Imagine stepping into the real world with a college diploma in hand, ready to embark on the exciting journey of your chosen career. But instead of feeling the sweet taste of freedom and accomplishment, you're shackled to a monumental burden – student debt. This debt crisis isn't just some random number on a financial statement. It is today's harsh reality facing millions of Gen Z individuals. A ball and chain of $30,000 or more are hamstringing you before you can even begin your life.

You will soon read the chapter "Reflections from Em," and her college experience and now "crippling debt." Across America, there are millions of similar stories.

This crippling handicap delays your ability to live life and reach milestones. A life-altering weight that shackles Gen Z's ability to thrive in the real world. Dreams of homeownership, entrepreneurial ventures, and financial independence are delayed or abandoned. The inability to reach these goals leads to constant stress churning in the pit of your stomach, making life feel empty and shallow, sometimes even affecting you physically. All because of loans you felt forced to take to complete your education.

Many Gen Z students feel disillusioned with the traditional path of higher education. The skyrocketing costs of tuition, combined with crippling student debt and a challenging job market. Many graduates cannot afford basic living expenses or make headway toward financial stability, much less financial freedom, even with their expensive degrees. It is both tragic and ironic that the very thing they went into such debt to obtain can't even help them get out of that very same debacle.

The truth is clear: students are being misled. They are told that expensive degrees will naturally lead to financial success, yet the reality is often sobering for many young adults. They are saddled with immense debt, unable to secure jobs that pay enough to justify the cost of their education. The system—-government policies, universities, and societal expectations—-has often failed them.

One state-sponsored college resource website says in BIG BOLD LETTERS: "Student loans can be a helpful tool to finance your education and achieve your career goals." Helpful??? They want you to take out expensive loans. We would go further than that and say they need you to take out student loans and want you to feel good about it. Schools push for subsidized student loans and meaningless degrees. Students are set up for failure. That helps the educational establishment and not you. This is just one of numerous examples of our self-perpetuating educational system. Do it their way, and you're crippled with debt. Do it your way, and you will have a chance to thrive!

The Numbers Speak for Themselves

According to Pew Research, one in four US adults under 40 have student loan debt. It is truly amazing to consider how pervasive these loans are.

> **$1.7 trillion:** That is the total amount of student debt in the United States. An incomprehensively large figure, and it continues to rise at an alarming rate.

> **44 million:** Number of Americans struggling to pay off their student loans.

> **11%:** The default rate on student loans is the highest of any debt category.

$30,000: Average student loan debt per graduate. The highest interest rate of any debt category.

The Wall Street Journal cited a Congressional Budget Office (CBO) study which indicated that most borrowers were making student loan payments inconsistently and only in small amounts. It was noted that "borrowers made payments greater than $10 in only 38 percent of the months." It's not uncommon for many graduates to be in default, forbearance, or deferment, as they cannot afford to make these payments and provide for themselves simultaneously. And that's not even considering those with children or other financial burdens.

Intuit Credit Karma reports (as of September 5, 2024) that 20 percent of student loan borrowers have yet to make any payments on their loans. This number rises to 27 percent among borrowers with a household income of less than $50,000. Also, this report said that 44 percent of Gen Z borrowers have depleted their savings to manage student loan payments.

These alarming statistics paint a stark picture of a generation burdened by financial obligation while they are just entering the workforce.

A podcaster recently asked seven students on campus from USC (University of Southern California): "How much debt are you in?" The interviewer discovered students with student debt/loans as low as $5k (total) to a high of $20k per semester (a Cinema & Media Studies major). The students with the lowest debt tended to take advantage of many part-time jobs. At sporting events, students cheer, "Fight On for ol' SC!" With the numbers present here, they should sing "fight, fight, fight against student debt!" and then taking the necessary steps to eliminate it.

According to a Federal Reserve Board survey, about one-third of student loan holders say the financial costs of their college degree outweigh the benefits.

Recent Loan Information

According to the Education Data Initiative, student loan debt has grown to $1.74 trillion as of 2024. Approximately 91% of which is made up of federal loans. The average cost of private higher education increased by around 12% between 2011-2021.

According to the U.S. Government Accountability Office:

Federal student loan payments resumed in October 2023 after more than 3 years of pause due to COVID-19. As of January 2024, the Education Department held $1.5 trillion in federal loans for nearly 43 million borrowers.

Of the borrowers whose loans had entered repayment and weren't in default:

> About half—accounting for about $706 billion in loans—were current on their payments.

> Nearly 30%—accounting for about $290 billion in loans—were past due on their payments.

The rest—accounting for about $254 billion in loans—were not expected to make payments because of deferment or forbearance.

Beyond Numbers: The Human Cost

Student debt is not merely a financial issue; it profoundly impacts the lives of individuals and society as a whole.

Research indicates a disturbing trend:

Delayed life milestones: Crippling debt forces many graduates to delay major life milestones, such as buying a house, starting a family, or saving for retirement.

Decreased economic mobility: The burden of debt hinders financial security and limits opportunities for wealth creation, perpetuating existing economic disparities.

Mental health strain: The constant stress and anxiety associated with debt can lead to depression, anxiety, and other mental health issues, impacting overall well-being. Students are struggling in other ways as well. According to a 2022-2023 Healthy Minds Study from the University of Michigan, roughly 40 percent of college students report suffering from a mental health disorder. This is not good at all and needs immediate attention.

Legal Action

On October 7, 2024, an antitrust class action lawsuit was filed in the U.S. District Court for the Northern District of Illinois against 40 private colleges and universities, including Yale, Stanford, NYU, Duke, Georgetown, and others. The action was brought for an alleged price-fixing scheme raising the cost of college. The plaintiffs were overcharged by $6,200 according to the suit.

One of the litigators said, "Those affected — mostly college applicants from divorced homes — could never have foreseen that this alleged scheme was in place, and students are left receiving less financial aid than they would in a fair market."

This legal action will be most interesting to watch moving forward.

Time to Cough Up the Cash

We recently came across an article entitled "6 Steps to Pay Back Student Loans Quicker" with a picture of a graduated student with a sullen expression dressed in full regalia. The depicted expression, with a frown, was undoubtedly realistic. It bespoke of unreadiness for the real world. We are not surprised. This undistinguished article suggests the first step should be to 'create a budget'. Brilliant! Exciting! To avoid feeling like the depressed graduated student noted in the article, students can proactively problem-solve by avoiding student loans in the first place. Our constant theme in this book!

Be Happy, Your Way

Pharrell Williams, the singer, songwriter, record producer, and fashion designer, is a member of Gen X and a dropout from Northwestern University after two years. About a year after the last member of Gen Z was born, his 2013 single, "Happy" rose to the top of the chart. A banger. "Clap along!" (1.3B YT views)

Gen X, also known as the forgotten generation, is the generation that has raised most of Gen Z.

This is the message that the educational establishment wants students to think, feel, and experience about all aspects of their college experiences: HAPPINESS. Skeptical? Ok. Just check out some posts and reels on IG from @commonapp and @reachhigher where everyone seems to be "super excited to apply to college." (Warning: the hopium there can be overwhelming at times).

Unfortunately, "Happy" often does not apply to the Gen Z educational experience. Unrealistic expectations, poor assumptions, misleading information, and lack of transparency work against students these days.

Especially after graduation. How could it? Graduates pay about $300 a month for a $30k student loan debt for a standard repayment plan. Many are not paying.

Gen Z college graduates do not think of this "Happy" song when paying for (or trying to pay) their student loans while also trying to pay for food, transportation, rent and more. Speaking of rent, Redfin Chief Economist recently said, "Many renters—especially young people—still feel the rent is too damn high." The average person's salary is eaten away by housing 26% and transportation 15%. It then becomes one massive budget squeeze for this generation. A squeeze with ongoing pain. Once the fun music stops, Gen Z college graduates know this financial reality too well when they check their email inboxes to pay the bills.

The Time to Act is Now

Gen Z faces a unique challenge – navigating the increasingly expensive world of higher education while entering a rapidly changing job market. This chapter serves as a wake-up call, highlighting the severity of the student debt crisis and its impact on young adults.

The Bottom Line

This chapter delivers a powerful message for Gen Z students: be wary of the student loan honey pot. It's a trap without any honey. Actually, not just be wary, but our recommendation is to avoid it at all costs. That is the path for ZERO COLLEGE DEBT, Gen Z.

The education system, aided by government policies, has set many young people up for failure by encouraging them to take on massive debt for degrees that often do not offer a good return on investment. The high cost of tuition, driven by limitless government-backed loans, has allowed universities to inflate their prices without providing better student outcomes.

Many graduates realize too late that they are burdened with insurmountable debt, entering a job market where their earnings do not justify the cost of their education. Students are sold a dream of financial success through college, yet the reality is far from that for many. High living costs, low wages, and overwhelming debt make achieving financial stability nearly impossible for recent graduates. It has forced barely hatched adults to work 2 to 3 jobs, take out more loans than they can afford, and live a life of pain and monotony.

This book passionately urges students to not just tap the breaks but hit the breaks before taking on student loans. For Gen Z, there are much better choices available. Alternatives like trade schools, community colleges, getting part-time jobs, real estate, or starting a business can offer more financially responsible paths. We emphasize reconsidering the "college or bust" mindset that has led many into financial ruin and highlight that success does not always require a traditional four-year degree. Be smarter about financial decisions and push back against a broken system.

The bottom line is clear: don't let the system trap you. Consider all options, avoid unnecessary debt, and take control of your financial future. If more students make these smarter choices, it can lead to a brighter, debt-free future for Gen Z.

Gen Z, you got this.

Chapter 03: College Today

Colleges, universities, professors, administrators, campuses, and students are all fascinating subjects today.

Over the years, millions of words have been written about the state of education in colleges and universities in this country. There are so many words, so much information, and misinformation, and so much noise that it's essential to understand what is true and how that truth works itself into decisions for your best interests.

For Gen Z, the challenge is to discern and understand the truth of today's college world as it applies to you and how you need to proceed. Students should view college decisions from an economic perspective as consumers and investors. This increases the educational and financial success for a Gen Z undergrad. Yet, many questions follow. Should I purchase this educational experience at this particular college? Should I invest in this major or degree? Should I buy the services this particular college offers? Should I invest my time and money in a given college for a solid return for my life and my future?

These supposedly enlightened universities generate many exciting stories, mixed messages, and policy decisions in today's academic world. The minimization and abolition of the SAT requirement and often the comparative ranking of high school GPAs (grade point averages) have occurred. This has been especially the case over the past three to five years.

Nearly 40% of all Americans over age 25 have a bachelor's degree. This percentage share has gradually eroded over recent years due to Gen Z's lack of acceptance of the college world.

Our main questions for Gen Z students in this book are: Should I go to college now or later? Should I forget about college altogether? Is going into debt worth it? What other paths should I consider?

If you do go to college, the smart move (and our strongest possible recommendation) is to graduate debt-free. That way you will have a professional asset in our portfolio (your college degree) and no future debt payments on your college loans. In finance, this is also known as *positive cash flow.*

So picture this: On graduation day, you experience a wonderful graduation ceremony with your family and friends, you will have no college debt, and hopefully a job offer in your pocket for future employment to launch your career.

Graduation day will be amazingly more wonderful with …. NO COLLEGE DEBT!!!

For college students today (or prospective students), college is not the same as it was for their older Millennial brothers or sisters, and certainly not the same as when (or if) their parents attended school.

No Cap

Over the past decade or so, the college and university worlds have changed significantly. We are tempted to use the word dramatically, but do not want to be accused of exaggeration.

In keeping with our Chapter 01: Straight Up promise of keeping it real and telling the truth, we are also obligated to mention the negative aspects of pursuing higher education.

Walton Family Foundation data shows that Gen Z students are 11 points less likely to say that they want to attend college than Millennials when they were twenty years old.

College enrollment continues to fall. "With the exception of wartime, the United States has never been through a period of declining educational attainment like this," said Michael Hicks at Ball State University's Miller College of Business.

Clearly, many headlines have not been university-friendly. A Wall Street Journal headline in May 2024 reported, "Test Scores Down, GPAs Up: The New Angst Over Grade Inflation." The WSJ reported that high-school grades were higher than before the pandemic. High school principals do not commend teachers for holding to high standards. There is more pressure to loosen many standards. Principals and superintendents with low failure rates in their schools get promotions and bonuses.

Yes, grade inflation is rampant everywhere: in high schools and in universities. In 2024, Western Oregon University leaders have announced plans to abolish D- and F grades for students. There are many other examples.

Student testing confirms these trends. The latest National Assessment of Educational Progress (NAEP) results show that 29% of 8th-graders are proficient in reading, and just 26% are proficient in math.

Much of this should not be that surprising. It only validates what students, parents, and educators see themselves. In a recent Gallup poll only 40% of Americans expressed "some" confidence in U.S. colleges and universities. Confidence among 18-34-year-olds has fallen to 22%. These are all new lows for academia.

Currently, about 40% of full-time university students in four-year colleges graduate on time. That number increase to 60% graduation in six years. Obviously, if you start, you want to finish.

It almost, it seems, that most college students are working on our PLAN C- Hybrid, by default or accidentally by circumstances.

Gen Z'ers have clearly recognized all these developments. They are asking: Where is the value in college today?

Bloated U.

Bloated university bureaucracies are everywhere. It has occurred at both public and private universities. One critic says schools are more concerned about safe spaces than actual learning. One writer politely called them non-academic office workers. There are organizational charts available online for some universities. Check it out, they are amazing.

For example, the University of Florida has 1 administrator for every 4 undergrads. At Yale, the ratio is a mind-boggling 1:1.

Harvard is currently home to 7,240 undergraduate students and 7,024 administrators, or nearly one administrator for each student. Harvard University is the first college in America, founded in 1636 by the Massachusetts Bay colonial legislature. We believe that in 17th century America, the curriculum was strong the student/admin ratio was not 1:1 at Harvard.

Teaching, preserving, and generating knowledge used to be the missions of our great universities. They eventually took it upon themselves to expand and re-define this core mission.

One harsh critic calls academia a rent-seeking scam. Harsh, indeed. These schools seem to prioritize their status and collecting your tuition money "without bearing any of the costs or risks that must be borne to achieve it."

The trend is the same for staff at elementary and secondary schools. Public school administrators have almost doubled since 2000, but the number of students is only up about 5%. One observer commented, "the bureaucratic state is undefeated."

No wonder protesters have taken to the streets to complain about college debt. They paid for these bloated bureaucracies without concern for student pocketbooks for years, even decades. If you were subsidized with a never-ending stream of college loans, where is the incentive to be lean, be efficient, and be cost-conscious?

Going back fifty-some years ago, in 1969, approximately 78 percent of faculty members in American universities and colleges held tenured or tenure-track positions. Now, that number is 20 percent, meaning that poorly paid adjuncts teach the majority of classes.

Colleges and Universities collectively have about a trillion dollars in endowments. Some universities have billion-dollar endowments worth the equivalent of some stocks on the S&P 500 stock index. And yet, tuition continues to climb year after year.

This is the college universe of today: bloated bureaucracies, tuition, and endowments.

The Impact of AI on Education and the Workforce

Looking ahead, the rise of artificial intelligence (AI) is shaping the future of education and employment. AI is expected to transform how students learn, offering personalized educational experiences through adaptive learning technologies. The workforce is also changing, with AI automating many jobs.

At the World Governments Summit in Dubai in February 2004, Nvidia CEO Jensen Huang made headlines when he said:

> "You probably recall over the course of the last 10, 15 years almost everybody who sits on a stage like this would tell you it is vital that children learn computer science. Now, it's almost the complete opposite."

Huang argued that the miracle of artificial intelligence allows for everyone to become a programmer. "It is vital that we upskill everyone," Huang said.

From a curriculum development perspective, will colleges and universities be able to keep up with the changes brought about by the AI revolution in the classroom? We shall see.

This book's chapter, AI Revolution, emphasizes that Gen Z was born at the perfect time to take advantage of this technological revolution.

Jobs after Graduation

A 2024 study by Burning Glass Institute indicated that 52 percent of college graduates are underemployed a year after graduation. And amazingly those who entered the job market underemployed, 73 percent stayed that way for ten years according to the research.

Data from the National Center for Education Statistics indicates that business degrees are the most popular major (19 percent) among college students today. The median annual salary for someone with a bachelor's degree in business is $65,000 (data from Coursera).

The second most popular degree is listed simply as "Health," at 13 percent.

If you don't break it down by major, then the average salary of a school's graduates doesn't mean much.

Surveys show that approximately half of all U.S. college graduates are working high-school-level jobs. This is sad, of course, but it also highlights the importance of selecting the best major to achieve the most value from your degree.

It is no wonder that employers today question the value of college degrees and turn to other factors to determine competency when searching for new employees. Soft skills such as curiosity, conceptual thinking and creativity have increasingly become important with new hire decisions.

Additionally, some say that trade or vocation schools (learning HVAC, welding, electronics or machinists skills) hold better value than universities.

Will College Pay off?

We say yes, but it is a *conditional* yes.

If you select the correct marketable major; a job market for that major, and other credentials you bring to the equation if you work part-time and if you avoid student loans (or pay them off while in college), then, our answer is absolutely YES. Especially if you leave with ZERO COLLEGE DEBT when you receive your diploma.

Again, think about it in terms of return on investment, such as ROI. If you leave school with zero debt, you can start your career without the need to devote up to 20% of your after-tax disposable income to student loans!

This question for prospective Gen Z college students should become personal: "Will college pay off for me?"

It will pay off very well if you leave campus with ZERO COLLEGE DEBT!

The equation is relatively straightforward if you want to reduce it to a formula: effort, motivation, focus, plus zero college debt will produce a big payoff.

Yet, many parents today say no. In some recent polls parents today say they DO NOT want their children to attend college.

Decades ago, the recommendation to prospective students was rather simple. Enroll in a high-quality, reasonably-priced college, select a major that fits your skills and interests, and finish your degree in four years. Sorry, but that is so pre-pandemic. It is very dated college admissions advice. Most students do not graduate within four years. Those students (Millennials and Gen X) who followed that one-size-fits-all recommendation may have graduated, but most graduated with a small mountain of student debt. Gen Z, follow a better path; follow your path.

The SAT is Back! (somewhat)

Over the past several decades, the SAT (and the ACT) have been under considerable attack by many. These anti-SAT voices have stated that the test is unfair, discriminates, and biased, and it is a poor measurement tool for colleges to use to evaluate student success. Those are just some of the complaints.

So much pressure has been put on universities that many schools raised the surrender flag and dropped the admissions requirement for these standardized tests altogether. Several Ivy League universities led the way.

Now, that trend is reversing itself at some of the more selective universities. The SAT and ACT are making a comeback.

Harvard, and several other Ivy League schools (Yale, Dartmouth, and Brown), have changed course and reinstated standardized testing for admissions. Students applying to enter Harvard in the Fall of 2025 (and beyond) will be required to submit SAT or ACT scores. The New York Times called it a "return to tradition."

Harvard cited a study by Opportunity Insights, which found that standardized test scores were a better predictor of academic success in college than a high school student's grades (GPA—Grade Point Average).

Another study, by Harvard and Brown professors, looked into standardized tests as a biased measure of student qualifications, stated: "But the data reveal that other measures — recommendation letters, extracurriculars, essays — are even more prone to such biases."

Currently, over 2,000 colleges remain either optional or completely free of standardized test requirements for incoming undergraduates.

What does all of this mean for Gen Z students? It means that for exclusive and highly selective universities (with low admissions rates) the SAT and ACT becomes important again. For most colleges that accept the majority of applicants, testing remains less important or unnecessary at all.

College Closures

Colleges are closing at an alarming rate, and it's not just a random, one-off trend. It is a result of deeper issues within the world of higher education itself. Colleges close several times per month, a sharp increase from previous years. Some schools are closing with little or no warning to students and parents. It is unthinkable not to feel terrible for the students, but they are in impossible situations. These closures are tied to declining enrollment, rising tuition costs, and shifting perspectives on the value of a degree.

We know that for Gen Z students, the traditional college path is becoming less appealing. Many are questioning whether it's worth the investment, considering the crushing student debt and the diminishing returns of a degree. Compared to Millennials, fewer Gen Z teens choose college as their primary route to success. Some are opting to work full-time, others are exploring entrepreneurial ventures, and dual enrollment in community colleges is rising.

During the last several years, many colleges in the U.S. have closed their door to students. According to a report by Best Colleges, more than 40 colleges have closed since 2020. Below is a list of some of the more recent school closures:

Lincoln College, Lincoln, IL

King's College, New York City

Holy Name University, Oakland, CA

Brightwood College, Van Nuys, California

Grace University, Omaha, NE

Iowa Wesleyan University, Mount Pleasant, IA

Wright University, Overland Park, KS

This unfortunate trend has caught many students and others by surprise. Some of the main reasons for these college closures include:

drop in enrollment (is the primary reason)

ransomware attack

removal of stimulus money (COVID-19 relief funds)

tuition not keeping up with inflation

poor university leadership and mismanagement

lack of philanthropy and alumni engagement

As noted, the rising costs of college are a significant factor. One educator said that college is the only industry that has seen a decline of economies of scale over time. Tuition has skyrocketed over the past two decades, making it harder for young people to justify the expense, especially when they see peers struggling with massive debt and minimal job prospects. Colleges, in turn, raised prices because student loans made it seem like the money was always available. But this has backfired, as many schools are no longer financially viable. When enrollment dropped by 10% or more at some of these smaller colleges, it produced a financial domino effect like a margin call on an investment account.

It is reported that only 47% of college students re-enroll in another college after a college closure.

Imagine getting your business degree at a school that went out of business!

If you are considering a small, private college to attend. It behooves you to do your research. Specifically, research includes asking questions about the financial soundness of that educational institution. It is now critical to perform your due diligence concerning small colleges.

Gen Z is waking up to the fact that higher education, in its current state, often doesn't deliver on its promises.

In short, many colleges are closing because they've priced themselves out of relevance for many young people. Gen Z isn't buying into the system like previous generations did. The question is: What will replace the traditional college experience?

Get a degree, Get wealthy

Median annual earnings of full-time, year-round workers ages 25–34 by educational attainment: 2020 (source: U.S. Department of Commerce)

Consider the following two numbers:

High school diploma $36,000

Bachelor's degree $59,600

There is no impressive bar chart here. Just two numbers. Numbers show the median earnings of workers according to two vital educational levels.

These are median income levels, meaning that 50% is above and 50% of the statistical population is below this number. This brings up many questions. Namely, how much better or worse (than the median) will you be in earning money? What will be the reasons or contributing factors? What skills will you be able to put to use? How motivated will you be? How creative and entrepreneurial will you be?

Question: "Is an Ivy League education worth it?" According to a 2023 Investopedia study their DCF (discounted cash flow) model says absolutely no. A public school delivers much more value, based upon overall returns, considering invested tuition and all other fees. Nevertheless, one piece of favorable news is that all of the Ivy Leagues schools offer substantial scholarships, financial aid, and merit scholarships for median income households.

Kenneth Fisher, a well-known money manager and founder of Fisher Investments (@fisher.investments), is interviewed frequently on business channels. During one recent interview he made some provocative comments about his firm's hiring practices. He said that in his "opinion going to a fancy name and school is an impediment to future success." Fisher said he prefers to hire candidates demonstrating common sense with a strong work ethic. His alma mater is California State Polytechnic University.

TAG in California

California has one of the most robust community college systems in the country. With over 100 campuses, students can easily find a program that works for them. One of the standout features of this system is the transfer pathway.

It would be shocking if a California high school or community college student were unfamiliar with the TAG program. Nevertheless, here is a brief description.

The Transfer Admission Guarantee (TAG) program is offered by the University of California (UC) system that guarantees admission to one of six UC campuses to eligible California community college students. The six participating UC campuses are Davis, Irvine, Merced, Riverside, Santa Barbara, and Santa Cruz.

[BTW - UC Berkeley, UCLA, and UC San Diego do not participate in the TAG program.]

So, suppose you are currently attending a school such as Foothill College or Modesto Junior College. In that case, you can graduate with a great degree from a school in the University of California (UC) system by utilizing the TAG program. This system allows students to skip the large, impersonal lecture halls that are common in the first two years at universities, jumping straight into upper-division, specialized courses. This not only saves money but also allows for a more focused academic experience. In fact, many top universities in California prefer transfer students from community colleges because these students have already proven they can succeed in college-level courses.

Is it cost-effective? Yes, indeed! Should students seriously consider it? Absolutely! If you live in California, this may be the plan for you to optimize your education and your future.

Bonus Tip: State U.

As emphasized, attending a state university (as an in-state student) can indeed be very beneficial from a tuition and cost management standpoint. Also, please be aware you may be able to save even more money if you attend a satellite campus of a public university, rather than the main university campus. It can be up to 40% cheaper. (This is not an option in all states, however).

The Future of Education

As Gen Z navigates a world with changing college landscapes, one thing is very clear: higher education is evolving. Whether it's AI transforming the classroom, alternative paths rising in popularity, or universities struggling to maintain relevance, your generation has more options and flexibility than ever before.

Admittedly, there were a lot of facts and data dumps in parts of this chapter. The objective here is not to build a case against attending college, an anti-PLAN A approach. The goal of this chapter is one of the book's primary goals. Gen Z must have a clear and realistic understanding of their educational, financial, and career choices and options. It is far too easy for students to have some kind of idealistic or even romantic view of college, solving all your dreams, desires, and wishes. That viewpoint has been sold to students by the educational system for far too long. That viewpoint is dated and counter-productive. If you want a fun and impractical college experience, select a school from a Top 10 Party Schools list and rack up your student loans. We can easily predict where that will lead you.

Today, there are a lot of headwinds working against motivated students who are interested in attending college after high school. Some of these issues have been identified in this chapter. If you choose college, your goal should be to graduate debt-free. Scholarships, part-time work, and strategic use of community colleges can make this happen. College isn't for everyone. Explore all your options, from trade schools to online certifications. You can still achieve great success without a traditional four-year degree.

Yes, picking up new skills and learning some wonderful courses is great. It is imperative for Gen Z to engineer their college education path with a realistic financial perspective and be able to answer how they expect to earn an ROI (return on investment) on their degree. Many in Gen Z have mastered this learning curve and are now wise at doing just that—examining the true value of a college education for themselves. Will you be among them?

Albert Einstein once said, "The value of a college education is not the learning of many facts but the training of the mind to think." In today's world, how and where you choose to learn will define your path, but one thing is sure: the ability to think critically, adapt, and innovate will remain essential to your future success.

Chapter 04: 404 (aka PLAN B)

A 404 error is an HTTP status code indicating that the webpage you were trying to reach could not be found on the site. The webpage could have been renamed to another URL or found no longer necessary. The page is simply missing online.

You, too, can go 404, MIA, or 86 (restaurant term) when it comes to your individual college admissions decision.

After graduating from high school, you don't enroll, attend, or show up for college. But this is not an error. You do this on purpose. You can't be found on campus since you are doing something else. Your status is MOC (missing on campus). You'll be doing your own thing, profitably. You'll be fine.

To be clear, this is PLAN B: Don't go to college. You choose another option, a different path. Only PLAN B is not an error; you do this on purpose because this is your best possible option. It is different from somebody else's best option for you. It is the best option for you. You are ditching the traditional educational script but keeping your options open. Viva PLAN B!

Go to work, begin your career, and become a freelancer, a solopreneur, a digital nomad, and your one-person business entity. You become your own brand.

If you want to go to college, you can always start several years later, if necessary. That is when PLAN B becomes PLAN C.

PLAN B: A Choice, Not a Backup

The term "PLAN B" often carries a negative connotation, implying a secondary or inferior option. However, this perception needs to be revised. For the purposes of this book, PLAN B is another choice, a path that may align better with individual goals and preferences. It's a reminder that there isn't necessarily one "right" way to pursue higher education. Whether it's a community college, trade school, a gap year, or no college, PLAN B can be the best choice for many students. By considering all available options and conducting thorough research, individuals can make informed decisions that align with their unique circumstances and aspirations.

Again, PLAN B means something other than that it is 2nd best or inferior to PLAN A. PLAN B is simply the best option for you now.

The Pandemic

Many Gen Z students voted with their feet regarding remaining enrolled in college during the pandemic. The loss amounted to a staggering one million fewer students compared to before the pandemic began (c.2022, National Student Clearinghouse Research Center). This was a historic fallout.

When it came to attending class during the pandemic, many students called it "Zoom school" (or worse, expressions). The idea of going to a college, especially at prestigious and expensive universities, and being forced to attend online classes because of the pandemic didn't sit right with many students (when they were first- or second-year students). They felt they were not receiving a valuable educational experience for their time and money. How could you feel otherwise under lockdown conditions? Many of these expensive schools have billion-dollar endowments. To pay top dollar tuition for an online classroom experience was not well received. Consequently, many students woke up and left college. Many educators worry that these students have gone for good.

Who can predict what the world of higher education would look like if another pandemic were to happen?

Gap year

Gap year, gap experience and gap semester are all the same concepts.

So, do you wanna ditch college? That is fine. It's not a one-way street: You can enroll later if you change your mind.

This personal strategy would be consistent with - PLAN B: do not attend college (permanently), or evolve into PLAN C: Hybrid solution. (i.e. Delay attending college for some time)

Consider a gap year (or two), a time of self-discovery, not a permanent goodbye to college. Be prepared for judgment, however. Our society is conditioned to love its college grads. Be ready to explain and defend your choice with confidence. Also, network like crazy: Building connections is crucial in any path.

Taking time off after high school means allowing the student (you) to do something better for themselves for the next year or more. It usually means something other than getting a job and beginning your career. Playing video games for a year does not fit the best gap year experience option.

"Gap year" has evolved to include more structured and purposeful activities. Gen Z is known for being pragmatic and socially conscious, so their gap years often involve travel, volunteering, internships, or other forms of experiential learning. Some programs offer immersive experiences that align with their values and goals.

Are you considering a gap year, or know someone who is?

If you are considering a gap year, we recommend speaking with several people who have had purposeful gap experiences.

College issues and questions

There are many reasons students leave college quickly or do not attend altogether. Listed below are a few of those reasons and circumstances.

Why do people leave college?

> health issues
>
> drug addiction
>
> mental illness
>
> financial, affordability issues
>
> to feel liberated
>
> disliked college

Why do people not go?

> joined the military
>
> went to flight school to become a pilot
>
> hated school
>
> no particular reason
>
> didn't want college loans
>
> woke culture issues
>
> free speech concerns

Admissions Craziness

Think about this fascinating illustration of today's bizarre world of college admissions.

This student's biography reads as follows: He is a top 2023 graduate of a prestigious high school in Palo Alto, California. He reported a GPA of almost 4.0. His SAT score? Also incredible: 1590/1600. In his leisure time, he started a website. The name of this student is Stanley Zhong.

Stanley submits 18 college applications, including ones to MIT and Stanford. Just two acceptances come back to his inbox: only the University of Texas and the University of Maryland will admit him. Pretty bizarre, no?

Stanley, however, has the final laugh. He accepted a job offer from Google as a full-time software engineer.

Unsane, no?

He didn't need a Google certificate on his resume to be hired (which is mostly a joke, anyway).

The bottom line is that more than a dozen colleges are missing out on Stanley's talents, but not Google.

So, what can we say? Stanley adopted PLAN B for his personal college strategy by accident—a fortuitous accident. Congratulations Stanley!

New School Startup

He dropped out of MIT, where he studied computer science and mathematics. He became the world's youngest self-made billionaire at age 24. Forbes says he is currently worth $2 billion. His name is Alexandr Wang (@alexandr_wang) and in 2016 he founded Scale AI, which annotates data in computer vision and audio transcription.

Wang is not just gifted academically, he possesses the emotional intelligence to run a successful business.

"I grew up in a small town in New Mexico called Los Alamos New Mexico," he said. His parents are military physicists. Smart genes run in the family.

He was also named to the Time 100 Next and Time100 AI lists.

Alexandr Wang is so very CEO.

You're right, Alexandr is not a typical student, and his successful startup is far from the norm. But, he had a dream and made it happen. What is your dream Gen Z?

Harvard Dropout

Another inspiring story is Sara Du (@saraduit), who describes herself as a self-taught engineer turned founder and Harvard dropout.

Better than Harvard, in our opinion, is that she graduated from the prestigious startup accelerator Y Combinator (@ycombinator). YC has launched more than 4,000 companies which are now valued at $600 billion.

Sara is the cofounder of AlloyAutomation (@alloyautomation), an embedded integrations platform used to simplify & accelerate all aspects of integration development. Her company has raised several funding rounds from prominent venture capital firms.

Fuhgeddaboudit

Not happy that her undergraduate experience at New York University during the pandemic devolved into the disappointing realities of Zoom University, pre-law student Rikki Schlott (@RIKKISCHLOTT) said - I'm out of here.

Unwilling to tolerate the lockdown measures, she decided to leave NYU and try journalism instead. She authored an article titled "Why I Joined the College Exodus," co-authored a book, and joined the New York Post as a columnist writing about higher education, women's issues, freedom of speech, and popular culture. Rikki is very open to letting her readers know what she thinks.

A High School Dropout Story

He is the youngest founder of a unicorn company (a billion-dollar startup). He dropped out of his Midwest high school and moved to the Bay Area. He started his company at 16 years old. He raised $128 million in 6 months from prominent venture capital firms.

His name is Samir Vasavada (@samir_vasavada). He co-founded Vise, a company that uses artificial intelligence (AI) to help wealth managers manage individual portfolios. Despite facing early failures, Samir's persistence paid off. Vise recently achieved a valuation of over $1 billion. Samir Vasavada's journey is indeed remarkable!

Samir says his company Vise is "fueling the trillion-dollar RIA aggregator revolution."

In an interview, Samir said that he used to think that the smartest people went to the best universities. But he discovered that was often not true. His direct hiring experiences taught him this. He said he prefers hiring problem solvers with the right customer mindset.

It's inspiring to see how he turned many challenges into success. Samir encourages "more young people to start businesses."

Let's be real here. Samir's story and journey are rare, no doubt. Nevertheless, the key learning point students can benefit from is understanding his laser-focused goal-setting and individual persistence. He put his PLAN B into effect on his terms.

Companies Not Requiring College Degrees

Several prominent companies are ditching the degree requirement for specific roles, including:

Tech Giants:

Google: Dropped degree requirements for several sales positions in 2021.

IBM: Removed degree requirements for some tech and customer service roles.

Apple: No longer requires a degree for some software engineering positions.

Dell: Offers "alternative paths to employment" for certain roles.

Microsoft: Focuses on skill-based hiring for various positions.

Other Major Companies:

Hilton: No longer requires a degree for many entry-level and mid-level positions.

Bank of America: Offers alternative pathways for entry-level jobs through its "Skillshare" program.

Tesla: Focuses on skills and experience over degrees for many roles.

Costco: Offers competitive salaries and benefits without requiring a degree.

Walgreens: No degree is required for various pharmacy technician positions.

Reasons Behind the Change:

There are several factors that contribute to this shift.

1. Labor Shortage: A tight labor market, especially in skilled fields, means companies expand their talent pool beyond degree holders.

2. Skill-Based Hiring: Employers increasingly focus on identifying specific skills needed for a job rather than relying solely on a degree.

3. High Cost of Education: The rising cost of college education makes it less accessible to many, creating a talent gap companies are trying to bridge.

4. Diversity and Inclusion: Ditching the degree requirement promotes a more diverse workforce by including talented individuals without access to higher education.

5. Focus on Potential: Companies recognize that potential and aptitude can be identified through assessments and experience, not just degrees.

6. Evolving Skills Landscape: The rapid evolution of technology and business demands that a workforce constantly learn new skills, making degrees less relevant to long-term success.

7. Alternative Education Options: The rise of bootcamps, online courses, and certifications provides credible alternatives to traditional college degrees.

This trend represents a significant shift in hiring practices, and it remains to be seen how widespread it will become remains to be seen. However, it underscores the growing importance of skills and experience over formal education in today's job market.

A survey conducted among 800 U.S. employers by Intelligent.com reveals that 45% of companies plan to eliminate the bachelor's degree requirement for some positions in 2024. Industries dropping the degree requirement include: information services 72%, software 62%, finance and insurance 61%.

A short list of jobs not requiring a college degree:

Real Estate Broker

Web Developer

Dental Hygienist

IT Support

Electrician

Construction Manager

Commercial Pilot

Sales Representative

Gen Z: The Toolbelt Generation

Gen Z is also called, by some, The Toolbelt Generation.

Many students are foregoing college and exercising their preference for skilled trades and blue-collar jobs over traditional four-year college degrees. This is Plan B at its purest and finest. Gen Z is rapidly joining blue-collar jobs such as plumbers, electricians, auto body repair, and HVAC techs. It is a seller's market. These high school grads are declining college to avoid student loans and other headaches associated with college attendance today. Gen Z's changing perceptions about blue-collar jobs are diminishing, and strong demand for these toolbelt jobs is real. More young people see these careers as viable and rewarding options.

Factors contributing to this trend:

1. Rising College Costs: The skyrocketing cost of tuition and the burden of student loans are major deterrents.

2. Job Market Opportunities: Many blue-collar jobs, such as electricians, plumbers, and construction workers, offer competitive salaries and benefits without requiring a college degree. Skilled trade salaries are competitive. For instance, new hires in construction are making more than those in some professional sectors. Many workers in the trades expect to make six-figure incomes after gaining experience.

3. Job Security: Skilled trades are in high demand due to labor shortages caused by retiring workers. Jobs like plumbing, electrical work, and welding are essential, making them recession-resistant.

4. Hands-on Work: For many Gen Z workers, the appeal lies in doing physical, tangible work rather than sitting behind a computer screen all day.

5. Entrepreneurial Potential: Many skilled trades offer paths to entrepreneurship, allowing workers to start their businesses, such as auto repair or custom bodywork.

Why This is Surprising to Many

This shift surprises some because of the long-standing belief that a four-year college degree is the gold standard for career success. There's still a stigma around blue-collar work, with many parents encouraging their children to attend college. However, Gen Z is beginning to question whether college is worth the high cost, especially when many college graduates end up in jobs that don't require their degrees.

Schooling Requirements for Toolbelt Jobs

Many toolbelt jobs don't require a traditional college degree. Instead, trade school, which often lasts a year or two, is sufficient. Programs typically cost far less than college, and many offer paid apprenticeships, where students earn while they learn. For example, welding programs may last nine months, while construction apprenticeships combine on-the-job training with classroom education. The best education for electricians is the IBEW.

Before publication we came across some interesting information about the welding profession. Formal schooling isn't always required to become a welder, but some training is essential. Some states or employers may require certification from organizations like the American Welding Society (AWS). Demand is high for welders. Nevertheless, be sure to research the health risks associated with this job. They can be significant.

Salaries in Skilled Trades

Salaries in the skilled trades are rising, often outpacing those in fields requiring a degree. Entry-level positions in construction, for instance, pay around $48,000 annually, and experienced tradespeople can earn six-figure incomes. By contrast, entry-level positions in professional services often pay less. Over time, tradespeople may still earn less than some professionals, but they start saving and earning earlier without college debt.

Are Gen Z Workers Happy with Toolbelt Jobs?

Yes, many in Gen Z report high satisfaction with their toolbelt jobs. In a survey, 94% of skilled tradespeople said they would encourage their children to follow the same path. These jobs offer a sense of fulfillment, hands-on work, and financial security—factors that resonate with a generation seeking meaningful work without the burden of student loans.

A Word of Caution

Realistically, even good jobs and opportunities do not guarantee rainbows and sunshine. So, too, with toolbelt jobs. Yes, Gen Z is turning to the trades instead of college. Yet, some jobs are physically demanding, and some have high turnover rates. For example, if you go into construction, you will get laid off for not producing enough. The wages can be excellent. However, work schedules can be demanding. Do your research and talk with those in the professions you are considering to make a well-informed career decision.

Ships Ahoy!

Here's a thought: How about joining the Navy instead? (instead of college) The Navy has made it more accessible.

In January 2024, changes occurred in the United States military enlistment criteria.

The United States Navy has taken a surprising turn of dropping all high school diploma and GED requirements for enlistments. This has raised concern and eyebrows. This is due to the recruiting crisis impacting all US military branches. Nevertheless, there is a caveat to this. Navy applicants need to score 50 or above on the ASVAB (Armed Services Vocational Aptitude Battery). This is a multiple-choice test that takes about three hours to complete.

The Navy is also promotes the possibility of earning a high school diploma to sailors as a benefit of enlisting. "Sailors who enlist under this policy change can achieve personal and professional growth by earning their GED while gaining experience in cutting-edge technologies and learning professional skills that allow them to exceed their expectations while serving in the Navy," it stated. Will this new recruiting sales pitch work with Gen Z?

In FY 2023, the Navy failed to meet its recruitment goal of 37,700 sailors, bringing in just 30,236.

Lastly, a recent study says that just 3% of Gen Z teens want to join the armed forces, down from 6% of Millennials who wanted to do so. The shortfall is substantial.

State Government Hiring Trends

In 2024, the governor of Massachusetts signed the order, titled "Instituting Skill-Based Hiring Practices," asserting that "skills-based hiring practices will strengthen the Commonwealth's workforce, increase access to quality jobs for nontraditional candidates with varied backgrounds and work experiences, and reduce structural barriers that result in inequities in pay and access to employment."

The document directs hiring managers to "consider the full set of competencies that candidates bring to the job beyond traditional education."

What does this mean? Massachusetts has cut the college degree requirements for 90% of state jobs. This is a recognition of present conditions and the realities of today's labor market.

This is an interesting development in Massachusetts since Boston has several highly-rated universities such as Harvard, MIT, and others.

This practice should not be considered that unusual. More and more government jobs don't require college degrees, and a liberal arts degree is no longer considered necessary or valuable to many government departments and agencies. Massachusetts is not an isolated case. Many states have similar laws and hiring practices.

For Gen Z, here again, the good news is that you can enter the workforce four years early and not be burdened by any college loans.

Conclusion: Navigating Your Own Odyssey

Although going to college is a common path, there are significant advantages and factors to consider for recent high school graduates who choose to start working right away.

The decision to forgo college is not a rejection of education but an assertion of individual agency, a declaration that success is not confined to traditional trajectories. Gen Z students standing at this crossroads are pioneers, shaping their destinies in a landscape of innovation, choice, and resilience. Whether it's entrepreneurship, vocational training, or a journey back to academia, the path is uniquely theirs. With its myriad possibilities, the world awaits the spirited footsteps of a generation unafraid to redefine success on their own terms.

Chapter 05: Talking about Gen Z

Several years ago, a Time magazine article was written entitled "How Generation Z Will Change the World."

We agree.

A year later, Forbes wrote, "Gen Z Is Already Changing The World," citing their "activism around gun control, immigration reform, and other causes."

This is true as well.

Gen Z is now thirty-four percent of the global labor force, the largest generation in history, and they know that.

We like using terms like pragmatic, tech-savvy, socially conscious, and value-driven to describe and capture Gen Z's essence. These descriptors also fit well with Gen Z's approach to college-related decisions.

Is it possible for Gen Z college students to graduate debt-free in today?

You're damn right it's possible. It's easier than ever before. It means a different path compared to previous generations of students. It means acquiring jobs or other sources of income. It also means not signing your good name on any student loan documents, thus avoiding the very tempting and easy money from the federal government. That easy and available money is not a gift. It must be returned with interest added on top. This is your borrowed money plus a lot of interest.

Gen Z

This book is written for and about Generation Z. More specifically, it is about the incredible educational and career choices Gen Z has before it.

For the purpose of this book, we are defining the year range of this generation from 1995 to 2012. (There is some modest flexibility as to these dates.) Gen Z succeeds the Millennials as a demographic cohort and precedes Generation Alpha.

Gen Z is a most interesting, complicated, and awesome generation. It is a misunderstood generation.

Gen Z has survived through (i.e. "been hit with") events such as COVID-19, the pandemic lockdown, record inflation, and the cost-of-living crisis. All this while considering whether to continue with their formal education after high school in a system that descends yearly.

Gen Z already knows who they are. But, as a review, and for others who are interested, Gen Z is known for the following attributes:

Diversity and Inclusion: Gen Z is the most racially and ethnically diverse generation yet. They value inclusivity and are more accepting of different races, genders, and sexual orientations. Gen Z students are drawn to colleges that emphasize diversity and inclusion. For instance, 78% of Gen Z students say that a college's commitment to social justice is important to them.

Digital Natives: Growing up with technology, they are highly proficient with digital tools and social media.

Pragmatic and Financially Minded: They tend to be practical, financially cautious, and value stability.

Socially Conscious: They are deeply concerned about social issues like climate change, equality, and mental health.

Individualistic and Authentic: They value authenticity and individual expression, often avoiding traditional labels.

Value for Money: Gen Z is very cost-conscious and often looks for colleges that offer good value for their tuition dollars. To minimize debt, they are more likely to consider community colleges, online courses, and in-state universities.

Focus on Career Readiness: This generation values programs that offer strong career services, internships, and job placement rates. They are interested in practical skills and real-world experience. A study by Handshake revealed that 85% of Gen Z students prioritize colleges with strong career services and internship opportunities.

Practical Skills: Gen Z is more likely to choose majors that offer clear career paths, such as computer science, business, and healthcare.

Interest in Technology and Innovation: Given their digital proficiency, Gen Z students are drawn to colleges with strong tech programs and innovative learning environments. 93% of Gen Z students believe that technology in the classroom is essential for their learning experience. They prefer colleges that offer online courses and digital resources. A survey by McKinsey & Company found that 74% of Gen Z students prefer a mix of in-person and online classes.

Social and Environmental Responsibility: Colleges that emphasize sustainability, social justice, and community service resonate well with Gen Z. They prefer institutions that align with their values and offer opportunities to make a positive impact. A survey by the Princeton Review found that 64% of Gen Z students consider a college's commitment to sustainability when making their decision.

Flexibility and Personalization: Gen Z values flexibility in their education, such as hybrid learning models and personalized learning paths. They appreciate the ability to tailor their education to fit their needs and interests.

Never stop learning and growing, Gen Z.

What Type of Decision?

Ok, Gen Z: do you see the college decision as primarily an investment or an educational decision?

Your decision has elements of both, of course, but primarily, which is it? We would argue it is an investment decision. But the college decision, as an investment decision, has dual purposes. First, there is quite obviously a financial element to it. Also, it is an investment in yourself as a person. It includes things like your career, learning, growing, etc. You become the brand—the brand of You Inc.

When we think of investments, we think of stocks, bonds, crypto, gold, and real estate. Those items are assets on our balance sheet. Managing liabilities is also extremely important. Gen Z, if you eliminate student loans as a liability, you automatically improve your net worth. The equation becomes simple and obvious. But this point about managing your balance sheet is more important than achieving a high FICO credit score.

A college degree is a type of asset as well. It is just not monetarily measured on a personal balance sheet. It could be an intangible asset similar to intellectual property. Relative to your college degree, the idea is to generate an ROI off of it - a return on investment. If you can generate a positive return while ACHIEVING ZERO COLLEGE DEBT, the percentage returns will begin to look very attractive.

Detractors

Since this book is committed to delivering the truth, we will continue with that philosophy in mind.

Yes, Gen Z you have your detractors. Not everyone loves your generation. But, you already know this.

Especially in the workplace, Gen Z is described as having a short attention span, being lazy, entitled, carefree, and worse.

As you are well aware, there are many non-fans of your generation, Gen Z. These detractors regularly write articles, blogs, and post comments on social media, adding to this so-called poor reputation. Gen Z is hit with many inaccurate stereotypes. A lot of this is just lazy journalism since the media tends to cycle through these same themes for every generation. (There is only one, The Greatest Generation.)

Detractors of Gen Z often resort to name-calling. You are called the slacker generation and worse. You are late for work, you hate the 9-5, and you think you are underappreciated. One writer wrote they are a "coddled, grade-inflated" demographic. Gen Z continues to be slammed. Despite the increased stress load placed on this generation, despite the ridiculous amounts of labor they have to endure because of the cost of living, they completely ignore these factors and continue to view the world through their lenses. With this perspective in mind, it is more clear as to the why behind Gen Z's lack of enthusiasm at times.

One might wonder how these non-fans of Gen Z are so fortunate to have minimal personal shortcomings or idiosyncrasies themselves. Perhaps they are projecting their near perfectionism when they were teenagers or in their twenties.

Sure, all generations have weird ones and poor performers. Yet, one of the things we admire is that Gen Z simply has different values and priorities. They dare to ask the question, "What's wrong with that?"

Some more examples include:

An Academy Award-winning actress recently said that Gen Z is "really annoying" and very lazy in the workplace.

One YouTube podcaster righteously proclaims that "Gen Z entitlement is staggering."

Blah, blah, blah ......

What is the reaction of the publishers of this book? It's more of the same old same old. These detractors don't understand that it is only a small minority. Plus, these negative comments say more about them rather than Gen Z.

One sensationalistic influencer says two-thirds of Gen Z are using TikTok as a search engine. (Gen Z makes up 60 percent of the app's users.)

It is easy to be a critic, especially these days, when everybody wants to be an influencer.

Many 9-5 jobs are overrated and doesn't necessarily match with the life goals and career objectives of many Gen Z'ers. So be it. Gen Z has more important things to be concerned about.

The authors believe that Gen Z will be very well adjusted overall in the long run. We are quite optimistic about this generation.

Let us conclude here by agreeing with Stanford University scholar Roberta Katz, who says that Gen Z is not 'coddled.' They are highly collaborative, self-reliant and pragmatic. (Based on her multi-year Gen Z research project funded by the Knight Foundation).

Gen Z, stay strong.

Gen Z, stay out of debt.

Got Rizz?

Rizz is Oxford's 2023 Word of the Year. The Oxford University Press publishing house said it is a colloquial noun defined as style, charm, or attractiveness.

For our purposes, we define it as charisma, although it has romantic connotations and other descriptions. This word is another example of Gen Z distinguishing itself from other generations.

The word went viral when Spider-Man and Uncharted actor Tom Holland (@tomholland2013) was asked about Rizz during an interview.

Does Gen Z have Rizz? Of course, it does. Rizz is another example of how Gen Z stands out from the crowd.

But while it is and was a fun and trendy term, it might not fully capture Gen Z's broader characteristics.

Chapter 06: Community College

Unlocking the Path to Success: The Benefits of Starting at Community College

Although well-known, community colleges in America continue to be among the best educational options available. With our Gen Z goal of a debt-free education, community colleges should be clearly considered. Often overlooked for various reasons, these institutions provide many advantages, making them a strategic and cost-effective option for a substantial proportion of Gen Z students. In fact, today, many community colleges are struggling to offer enough classes to meet the increased demand.

The escalating cost of higher education has caused many Gen Z students to actively seek alternatives that deliver a good education without the crippling burden of debt. Unfortunately, many students have been misled about the value of community college even by friends and family members.

By attending community college this would be your choice of electing to go with - PLAN A: attend college (after high school) decision, or even PLAN C: Hybrid solution (delay attending college). Think about it. If you secure a part-time job, while attending school, you can potentially leave community college with a solid handful of college credit hours with zero college debt and no student loans. That would be truly golden.

For many high school graduates in the United States, the first step toward higher education is deciding where to start their academic career. While traditional four-year universities are typically mentioned as aspirational destinations, an increasing number of students understand the value of completing a community college before transferring to a larger institution. Enrolling in a community college before attending university provides multiple advantages, including financial, personal, and educational rewards that put students on the path to success.

Unlocking the value proposition

Community colleges offer a variety of advantages that traditional four-year universities often struggle to match:

1. Financial savings: a cost-effective approach.

One of the most appealing arguments for attending community college is the significant cost savings it offers. Community colleges offer much lower tuition than four-year universities. The average annual tuition at a community college in the United States is roughly $3,800, compared to more than $10,000 for in-state students at public four-year universities and approximately $37,000 for private institutions. Thousands of dollars can be saved. Tuition is frequently more than half the cost of public four-year universities (in-state). Students who spend their first two years at a community college can finish many of their baseline and necessary courses at a cheaper cost, making higher education more accessible and affordable.

This cost advantage allows Gen Z to:

Avoid student loan debt: By completing the general education curriculum and prerequisites at a community college, students can significantly reduce their overall educational costs or eliminate student loans altogether.

Maximize financial aid: Community colleges usually provide generous financial aid packages that include grants, scholarships, and work-study opportunities, reducing students' financial burden. This is real and can be substantial.

Invest in future career goals: The money saved by attending community college can be used to fund additional educational pursuits, such as specialized certificates or graduate school programs.

2. Academic preparedness facilitates a smoother transition.

Starting at a community college allows students to become accustomed to the obligations of college life. It's a wonderful platform for building a solid intellectual foundation. Students can take introductory and prerequisite courses at their own pace, ensuring that they are well-prepared for the demands of university-level education.

Additionally, community colleges often provide smaller class sizes, resulting in a more personalized learning environment. Smaller class sizes allow students to engage more directly with professors, many of whom also teach at top-tier universities. These professors often choose to work at community colleges because they genuinely care about teaching, not just conducting research or chasing tenure. Professors are usually more personable making academic transitions easier and providing important support to students. Finding and hiring the best teachers at community schools can be easier in many circumstances.

3. Flexibility and Exploration: Academic Diversity.

Community schools offer a wide variety of academic programs and courses, allowing students to explore several areas of interest without committing to a certain major prematurely. This versatility is useful for students who are unsure about their career path or want to try out other professions before making a final decision.

Furthermore, community colleges are well-known for offering vocational and technical programs that educate students for careers in high-demand areas, allowing them to enter the job market upon graduation.

Community colleges frequently offer online courses, which can be a useful choice for students who must study remotely or have unpredictable schedules. Online classes also allow students to work at their own pace, making it easier to balance their coursework with other responsibilities.

4. Transfer agreements: A Smooth Transition.

Community colleges commonly form articulation agreements with four-year universities. These agreements ensure that credits earned at the community college transfer seamlessly to the larger university, provided the student meets certain academic requirements. Some community colleges have guaranteed admission programs with state universities (e.g., California), giving students a clear path to a four-year degree.

In California 18,245 community college students transferred to University of California college campuses in 2022-23 (source: UC Data Warehouse).

Earning a two-year degree before pursuing a bachelor's degree has become the smart choice and strategy for many students. We cannot emphasize this enough.

This allows students to:

Complete required courses at a lower cost: Earn credits at a community college and transfer them to a four-year institution, saving money on expensive upper-division classes.

Take starting classes in a range of areas to discover new interests and develop career goals before enrolling in a four-year university program.

Maintain flexibility and affordability. While attending a community college, also consider taking part-time or online classes to boost flexibility and possibly lower living expenses.

5. A varied student body offers a broad cultural experience.

Community colleges often have a varied student body that includes people of many ages, nationalities, and life experiences. This diversity enriches the classroom environment by exposing students to various ideas while also developing a sense of community and inclusiveness. Most students have jobs, expenses, and families to consider.

6. Beyond cost savings, a conducive environment for academic success.

Community colleges provide a supportive and personalized learning environment that encourages a sense of belonging while encouraging academic success. This beneficial atmosphere contains the following:

Small class sizes: Receive individualized attention from dedicated educators who provide personalized advice and assistance.

Access tutoring centers, writing labs, and academic advisors to help you succeed in your studies.

Diverse student population: Connect with peers from all backgrounds to create a dynamic and inclusive learning environment.

7. Challenging Stigma: Changing Community College Perceptions.

Unfortunately, some people think community colleges are inferior to four-year institutions. The reality is that this stigma is no longer as true or as accurate as it was few years ago. However, it is vital to overcome this stigma and recognize the specific advantages these colleges offer. Gen Z's practicality and emphasis on value are altering attitudes. Students now appreciate the economic and academic benefits of community institutions, opening the way for a more balanced and informed approach to higher education.

Community colleges provide a valuable and affordable educational pathway, allowing individuals to:

Gain practical skills and information: Learn the skills and knowledge required for a transfer or entry into the workforce.

Investigate job opportunities: Use career counseling programs and internships to gain practical experience and explore various career paths.

Improve your work prospects: Acquire relevant skills and certifications that employers value, increasing your employability and earning potential.

To recap, the benefits of attending community college before transferring to a higher education institution are both tangible and intangible. It not only saves students money, but it also allows them to make a smoother academic transition, pursue their hobbies, and be a part of a welcoming community. By making this strategic decision, students can start their journey to success in higher education while reducing financial hardship and maximizing personal and educational rewards. The community college experience emphasizes that the journey to a university degree is about more than just the destination, but also the important steps taken along the way.

Seizing the Opportunity: Maximizing Your Community College Experience

To maximize your success at a community college, also consider these personal strategies:

Set Clear Goals: Define your academic and career objectives from the outset to guide your course selection and ensure that your studies align with your ambitions.

Use Support Services: To navigate the academic environment and make the most of your learning experience, seek help from academic advisers, career counselors, and tutors.

Connect with your peers. Building relationships with other students fosters a sense of community, provides a support network, and enhances the overall educational experience.

Get involved in university activities: Join organizations, groups, and extracurricular activities to obtain leadership experience, explore your interests, and develop a strong résumé.

Network with Professionals: Internships, volunteer work, or guest lectures can help you gain practical experience and insights into your business.

Gen Z can adopt this strategic path to achieve their educational goals without incurring excessive debt by recognizing the value proposition of community schools, taking advantage of their unique benefits, and actively participating in the academic and social environments.

Free community college

As of the publication date of this book, 33 U.S. states offer some form of free community college to their students. That is more than half the country! However, it is important to note that the specific features of these programs vary by state, including:

Eligibility: Some programs admit all students, while others have economic, residency, or academic performance criteria.

Coverage: Some programs only cover tuition, whilst others include fees, textbooks, and other expenses.

Duration: Some programs offer free tuition for two years, while others just cover one year or semester.

This is the list of the 33 states that offer (some form of) a free community college:

Arkansas: AR Futures Grant

California's College Promise Grant

Connecticut: Pledge to Advance Connecticut (PACt)

Delaware: Delaware Promise

Georgia: Hope Grant and Zell Miller Scholarship

Hawaii: Hawaii Promise Scholarship

Indiana's 21st Century Scholars Program

Iowa: The Last Dollar Scholarship

Kansas: Kansas Promise Scholarship

Kentucky: Work Ready Kentucky Scholarship

Louisiana: Louisiana Promise

Maine: The Community College Promise

Maryland: Maryland Promise Scholarship

Massachusetts: The Commonwealth Promise

Michigan: Reconnect Scholarship

Missouri: A+ scholarship

Montana's University System Promise

Nevada: The Nevada Promise Scholarship

NJ: Community College Opportunity Grants (CCOG)

New Mexico's Lottery Scholarship

New York: Excelsior Scholarship

North Carolina: NCSSM and the NC Community College Promise

Oklahoma: The Reach Higher Act

Oregon: Oregon Promise

Rhode Island: The Rhode Island Promise Scholarship

South Carolina Lottery Scholarship

South Dakota: South Dakota Promise

Tennessee: The Tennessee Promise

Vermont: Vermont Promise

Virginia's Community College System Promise

Washington: College-bound Scholarship

West Virginia's Mountaineer Hope Scholarship

Wyoming: The Wyoming Hathaway Scholarship

It is crucial to research the specific program in your state to see if you are eligible and what it covers. Furthermore, many programs may impose conditions or restrictions, such as maintaining a certain GPA or taking a set amount of credits per semester. Each application should be thoroughly investigated to determine its details and any limitations. More information is typically accessible on the website of your state's department of higher education or the community college where you want to enroll.

Unfortunately, there are no free community college programs in Pennsylvania, Florida, Texas, or Arizona, among other states.

Top Community Colleges in the United States

The good news is that we are really fortunate to have numerous very good and even great community colleges in many locations across America.

The following is a list of top institutions that appear on numerous rankings lists for the best community colleges in the country. If none of these colleges are in your home state, we are confident you will find a community college to fit your educational goals. Many of these schools have low student-faculty ratios, excellent graduation rates, and low (or even free) tuition.

Bellingham Technical College; Bellingham, Washington.

Atlantic Technical College, Coconut Creek, FL

Southeast Technical College in Sioux Falls, South Dakota

Foothill College in Los Altos Hills, California

Las Positas College in Livermore, California

Santa Barbara City College in Santa Barbara, California.

Fox Valley Technical College in Appleton, Wisconsin

Northwood Technical College in Rice Lake, Wisconsin

A podcaster recently interviewed students at Orange Coast Community College, in Costa Mesa, CA, well known for its strong programs in marine science and aeronautics. Students were asked how much they pay for classes. One said $50 per class, another said about $500 per semester (depending upon grants and awards). Community college is free for many students in California. It's important to check with the specific community college you're interested in to understand their offerings and eligibility criteria.

Some Caution

Moving forward, as clearly noted, attending a community college is a great way to save money while completing your freshman and/or sophomore years. One disadvantage of attending a community college is that not all students fit in (relative to their commitment and level of seriousness). Most community colleges require only a high school diploma or GED to enroll. Some students in class do not read the materials assigned to them or do any class-related homework. It's grade 13 for them and it's almost like they're continuing their high school experience at a new campus location. As a new freshman, it's easy to get preoccupied and get associated with the wrong influence. When you research and consider a university with a reasonable admittance rate, the students are significantly more serious about their college studies. If you are a serious student enrolling in a community college, you must stay focused. Focus on your studies, get your credit hours, get your required courses out of the way, save money, and move on to the university.

Why Gen Z Should Consider Community College

Gen Z is known for valuing flexibility, practicality, and financial independence. For many, community college checks all those boxes. The ability to explore different academic interests, avoid crushing debt, and build practical skills while studying makes community college an attractive option.

One student, who attended Northern Virginia Community College, said in her podcast, "honestly it was just the best option for me because what a lot of people don't realize is that you save so much money. It's insane the amount of money you save going to community college and that was definitely the number one reason why I chose to go there."

Moreover, in today's job market, employers are increasingly looking for real-world experience over prestigious degrees. Internships, work experience, and practical skills gained through flexible community college schedules can often outweigh the brand name on a diploma. Choosing community college does not show weakness; rather, it demonstrates resourcefulness, financial responsibility, and a desire to achieve academic success on your own terms.

So far, in 2024, enrollment in community college is up 4.7% which is the fast annual growth since prior to the pandemic.

So, is community college right for you? If you're looking for a cost-effective way to start your higher education journey, want the freedom to work while studying, or just need some time to figure out your career path, community college might be the perfect fit. Whether you choose to transfer to a four-year university or not, community college offers the education, flexibility, and opportunities that align with Gen Z's forward-thinking approach to life and career.

Go for it, Gen Z. You will not regret enrolling into a community college. This a big part of the secret sauce successfully leading students to a Zero College Debt world.

Celebrities and famous people who attended community college

Many celebrities and famous people have attended U.S. community colleges before achieving fame. Here are a few notable examples:

Tom Hanks - The Oscar-winning actor attended Chabot College in California before transferring to California State University, Sacramento.

Morgan Freeman - The acclaimed actor studied at Los Angeles City College.

Aaron Rodgers - The NFL quarterback attended Butte College in California before transferring to the University of California, Berkeley.

Halle Berry - The actress attended Cuyahoga Community College in Ohio.

Guy Fieri - The celebrity chef attended American River College and College of the Redwoods in California.

Gabrielle Union - The actress attended Cuesta College in California.

Amy Tan - The author of "The Joy Luck Club" took classes at San Jose City College.

Eileen Collins - A retired NASA astronaut attended Corning Community College in New York.

Chapter 07: Gen Z Quiz

Students, please take the following quiz and respond honestly to the questions.

Q1: If it was absolutely necessary that you would graduate from college in 6 years, rather than 4 years; yet with no student loan debt or any other debts, would you agree to it?

Yes / No

Q2: If it was required of you to attend community college for two years to eventually graduate college with a bachelor's degree with no debt, would you do it?

a. Yes

b. No

c. Probably not

d. Not sure

e. Depends

Q3: If you needed to work full time or part time for six years to graduate college with no debt, would you do it?

Yes / No

Q4: Would you attend a State University in your home state, despite personally always disliking the school and despising their mascot and sports teams, providing they awarded you with scholarships which would you to graduate debt free at the time of picking up your college diploma?

Yes / No

[This is a quiz to test your seriousness, your overall mentality, and commitment to the goal of graduating with zero student loan debt or any other kind of college related debt.]

Answer key (correct answers)

Q1: Yes

Q2: Yes

Q3: Yes

Q4: Yes

Grading:

4/4 correct answers: **PASS**

One or more answers, wrong: **FAIL**

Oh, did we forget to tell you this was a PASS/FAIL quiz?? Welcome to the real world.

If you failed the test, you can retake it up to ONE time before you PASS. This is on the honor system.

If you got one or more questions wrong, it shows that you have a poor attitude or the goal of zero debt isn't that important to you (or both).

What does it matter if you graduate in 4-8 years; but have no debt???
Today, that is typically called one helluva accomplishment!!!

Think of this in terms of your own personal balance sheet. Your asset is
your bachelor's degree, and your student debt is $0 on the liabilities side
of your balance sheet. Your net worth is the difference between assets
and liabilities, btw.

Chapter 08: Meet Em

"Reflections from Em"

by Em

[Before, during and after college]

Hey there, I'm Emily, I go by Em (she/her). The publishers thought it'd be rad for me to spill the deets on my crazy journey. Buckle up, 'cause this is about my crippling debt rollercoaster.

So, I'm 26, trying like hell to adult like a boss. I'm told I'm healthy, attractive, a smarty, all that jazz. Born in Pennsylvania, but I'm now a wanderer in the Midwest. Stuck in a beige life, drowning in a sea of "what ifs." Not close to getting wifed up, got a not-so-serious boyfriend, and I've got this one-bedroom haven where I can think things over. By day, I'm rocking retail, saving a measly fifty bucks a month if the universe aligns in my favor. (Spoiler alert: it rarely does.) Yeah, retail. Don't judge. Better than dealing with a hundred idiots a day, with headphones crushing my brain cells, at a soul-sucking call center.

A couple of years back, I tossed my cap in the air, celebrating my liberal arts degree from a state school in PA. Let's call that the beginning of my solo decision-making journey. The college itself was cool, but the major? One of those that's on the "Worst College Majors" list. I was too intelligent to fall for those lists, so I mocked them. Fast forward, and here I am, $100 away from financial meltdown, if my car decides to throw a fit.

High school was golden and carefree. Drama club and epic acting roles, cool articles written for the school paper, my popularity oozing. Good grades flowed, mainly because I dodged math and science like the plague. College choices were abundant, and my auntie kicked in five grand for the cause. Sweet, right? Fans paying off. The rest? Loans. Easy peasy – sign, forget, pay later when you're eventually swimming in cash. My dreams were in place.

But oh, now the hindsight. No scholarships considered, campus living all the way, zero part-time jobs, and a lifestyle that screamed YOLO. Friendships, road trips, events – college had it all. A time for connections, adventures, and so much more. I've got some killer pictures! Ads, influencers, societal pressures and lack of financial education fueled my choices. The system is rigged - is my completely honest opinion.

Then came the "collection notices" arriving my senior year - that's what I called my advance warning letters about my upcoming monthly loan payments. I dubbed them my "future troubles," and that first shock letter made me drown my sorrows in whatever liquid courage was handy. Those loan warning notices kept coming faster than I could yell "SHIT!!!" in my empty dorm room. When I signed off on those loan docs, they were always really confusing and I never got the support or guidance I needed. Always facing dead ends.

"Shoulda Woulda Coulda" echoed in my head. Community college never crossed my mind, scholarships were never applied for, a part-time gig wasn't for me, frugality - nada; all of these things could've saved me. Yeah, a lot of missed opportunities and I really didn't sacrifice. But, alas, four years whizzed by, and there I was, a fresh grad catapulted into the REAL WORLD. It had to happen sometime.

My new diploma, my graduation bash, and then a not-so-great retail job in a big city. Now, I'm typing this story in my humble abode, single and pet-less due to unaffordable vet costs. Angry at my student loans? Hell yes. Angry at myself? Double yes.

No, it's not a six-figure school debt, but it's close, and on my retail grind, it might as well be. Every loan payment feels like I'm tossing dollars into the city sewer. Yeah, there was a payment delay during the pandemic. So frickin' what. Right now I have no budget. I make it, I spend it.

A while back, I joined up with some street protests against "the college debt crisis." Got some Apple Cash dollars paid by some group to carry a sign and yell chants into the void; I even made the newspaper. But I felt like a loser. (L: loser hand gesture on my forehead) Voting for politicians promising change in student debt? Empty promises. Going nowhere.

So here I am, slinging resumes, hoping for a miracle. My resume might be as dull as my life, who knows? There's a promotion in the pipeline at work – an extra $120 a week before taxes with the manager title. Woo-hoo! rolls eyes.

Get a law degree? Nah, I'm good. Too much agony and more debt there. Grad school? Meh. Launch an Instagram or TikTok channel? Doing what? I need to influence myself.

Yeah, I'm stressed, there is a lot of financial pressure and fear. Sleepless nights and other struggles. But let me tell you, some of my friends got it worse. "The 9-5 is the biggest f*cking scam out there," they say. I agree, but I just need a break. Get this, one of my dormmates from State U. is living in her car, wandering the west coast aimlessly, doing the nomad thing. Yeah, envision that.

Moral of this chaotic tale? Tiny mistakes snowball into a BIG FAT STUDENT LOAN DEBT. "Welcome to the club, Em." The system failed our generation. We're a force of millions. It's a call to action and there's power in self-awareness. I am determined to forge my own path.

Keep it real,

Em

[Note: Individual name(s) are fictitious and schools were not mentioned for privacy reasons]

Chapter 09: Idea$

Yes, Gen Z, this chapter is entitled "Idea$," which may sound enticing at first, but it is really about getting to work. Specifically, YOU are getting to work so that you don't have to choose the dreaded debt option. To repeat ourselves repeatedly: The goal is to avoid college loans or college debt of any kind. If that also becomes your goal, then certain sacrifices and choices need to be made. Any short-term pain you experience with part-time or full-time employment will be more than worth it in the long run. That is guaranteed.

We named Chapter 01: Straight Up. Other titles under consideration were "No Cap" and "Getting Real." This author attempts to tell students the truth about today's choices and decisions about college financial matters.

Your approach and mentality must differ from 90% of the other college students who will not make these plans. The other students will avoid the short-term pain associated with getting a job because it is just too easy to sign off on student loans year after year. Think of student loans as a medication that eases the pain of not immediately coming up with the total cost of college out-of-pocket, out of your pocket.

You will be approaching it differently since you are aware of the long-term benefits of this approach, and you will be highly grateful to your younger self for having the intelligence and maturity to make this work.

Ideas for Sources of Income

We need to be honest and blunt here, Gen Z; many of these ideas are standard and obvious. Nevertheless, having this list in place to review and consider for your income-generating ideas will be good. It is cash flow time for college!!!

Gen Z college students can explore many ways to earn or make money while in school. Here is a long and detailed list of potential income sources to consider:

Part-Time Jobs: Many college towns offer part-time job opportunities in retail, restaurants, or customer service. Typically pay minimum wage to slightly above minimum wage, depending on the employer and specific job responsibilities.

On-Campus Jobs: Look for on-campus jobs like working in the library, administrative offices, dining services, or as a teaching assistant. Similar to part-time jobs, ranging from minimum wage to slightly higher based on the position.

Work-Study Programs: Apply for federal work-study programs that provide part-time employment for students with financial need. Pay can vary, usually in line with federal or state minimum wage standards.

Freelancing: Utilize skills in writing, graphic design, web development, or digital marketing to find freelance gigs. Earnings can range widely based on the type of freelance work and expertise. Beginners might start at lower rates but can increase significantly with experience.

Tutoring: Offer tutoring services to other students in subjects you excel in. Hourly rates can vary widely, ranging from $15 to $50 or more depending on the subject and level of expertise.

Campus Ambassador Programs: Work as a brand ambassador for companies that target college students to promote their products or services.

Internships: Seek out paid internships related to your major or career interests. Paid internships can vary greatly, but many offer hourly wages or stipends ranging from minimum wage to higher rates, especially in specialized fields.

Research Assistant: Assist professors or researchers in their projects and get paid for your contributions. Compensation often depends on the project and funding but can range from $10 to $25 per hour or more.

Gig Economy Jobs: Explore gig economy platforms like Uber, Lyft, or food delivery services (Grubhub, DoorDash) for flexible income. Earnings fluctuate based on hours worked and demand but can range from $10 to $25 per hour, sometimes higher during peak times, depending on location and hours worked.

Sell Class Notes: If you're a good note-taker, you can sell your class notes to fellow students. Accept market rates or negotiate your best rate.

Sell Unused Items: Sell old textbooks, electronics, or clothing on online platforms like eBay, Amazon, or Poshmark.

Online Surveys and Market Research: Participate in online surveys and market research studies for compensation. Usually pay a few dollars to tens of dollars per survey, depending on the length and complexity.

Blogging or Vlogging: Start a blog or YouTube channel and monetize it through ads, sponsorships, and affiliate marketing. Income can vary widely from a few dollars per month to thousands of dollars per month, depending on audience size, engagement, and monetization strategies.

Pet Sitting or Dog Walking/Babysitting: Offer pet care services for local residents. Babysit for families in your community. Hourly rates typically range from $10 to $20, but can be higher for specialized services or certifications.

House Cleaning or Yard Work: Offer house cleaning, gardening, or lawn care services. Rates can vary widely based on location and services offered but may range from $15 to $50 per hour.

Photography: If you're a skilled photographer, you can take photos at events, parties, or for local businesses. Rates vary significantly based on the event, client, and expertise. Event photography might range from $50 to several hundred dollars per hour.

Sell Crafts or Artwork: Create and sell handmade crafts, artwork, or digital designs on platforms like Etsy or Redbubble. Income varies widely based on the item's popularity, quality, and marketing efforts.

Music or Performing Arts: If you have musical or performance talents, consider busking or performing at local events. Earnings depend on the gig, audience, and experience, ranging from a few dollars for small performances to hundreds or more for larger events.

Mobile Car Wash: Offer mobile car washing services to busy students and faculty. Prices range from $20 to $50 per car, depending on the services provided.

Remote Customer Service: Find remote customer service jobs that allow you to work from your dorm or apartment. Hourly rates typically range from $10 to $20 per hour for entry-level positions, potentially higher for specialized roles or experience.

Event Staff: Work as event staff at concerts, sports events, or conferences. Rates vary widely based on the event and responsibilities, typically ranging from minimum wage to $20 or more per hour.

Fitness Training: Become a certified fitness trainer and offer personal training sessions. Earnings can vary significantly based on location and client base, with rates ranging from $30 to $100+ per hour for personal training sessions.

Language Tutoring: Offer language tutoring services to students looking to improve their language skills. Rates often range from $15 to $50 or more per hour, depending on the language and level of expertise.

Tech Support: Assist people with computer or tech-related issues. Hourly rates can range from $15 to $30 or more, depending on the complexity of the issues being addressed.

Ridesharing: Drive for ridesharing services like Uber or Lyft. Earnings typically range from $10 to $25 per hour or more, depending on location, demand, and hours worked.

Rent Out Your Space: If you have extra space in your apartment, consider renting it out on platforms like Airbnb. Income can vary widely based on location, property type, and demand, potentially ranging from a few hundred to several thousand dollars per month. Coliving renting is booming.

Virtual Assistant: Provide administrative and organizational assistance to businesses and entrepreneurs. Rates vary based on services offered and experience, typically ranging from $15 to $50 or more per hour.

Remote Content Writing: Write articles, blog posts, or content for websites and online publications. Rates vary widely, but freelance writers often charge between $0.03 to $0.50 or more per word, depending on the project and expertise.

Podcast Production: Offer podcast editing, transcription, or production services. Rates may range from $20 to $100 or more per hour for editing, transcription, or production services.

Print on Demand: Create custom designs for apparel and merchandise and sell them through print-on-demand services. Income varies based on sales volume and product pricing, with potential earnings ranging from a few dollars to thousands per month.

Social Media Management: Manage social media accounts for small businesses or individuals. Rates can vary widely, but monthly retainers may range from a few hundred to several thousand dollars based on the services provided.

Delivery Services: Offer delivery services for local businesses or restaurants. Hourly rates may range from $10 to $25 or more, depending on the type of deliveries and location.

Event Planning: Plan and coordinate events for organizations or individuals. Income can vary widely based on event size and complexity, with rates often charged as a percentage of the event budget or as a flat fee.

Personal Shopping: Offer personal shopping services to people who need assistance with their purchases.

Consulting: If you have expertise in a specific area, consider offering consulting services in your field. Rates can vary significantly based on expertise and industry, with consultants charging anywhere from $50 to $300 or more per hour.

App Development: If you have coding skills, work on app development projects. Income can vary widely based on project complexity, scope, and client requirements. Rates can range from a few hundred dollars to tens of thousands or more for larger projects, depending on the app's functionalities and features.

Drop shipping: Start an online store and use drop shipping to sell products without holding inventory. Income can vary significantly based on the products sold, marketing efforts, and profit margins. Drop shippers can potentially earn from a few hundred to thousands of dollars per month or more.

Remote Data Entry: Find data entry or transcription jobs that you can do online. Hourly rates may range from $10 to $20 or more, depending on the data entry job's complexity and volume.

Mystery Shopping: Participate in mystery shopping programs to evaluate businesses and get paid for your feedback. Payments can vary based on the assignment, typically ranging from a few dollars to $50 or more per assignment, plus reimbursements for purchases.

Product Testing: Sign up for product testing and review opportunities. Compensation can range from receiving free products to monetary payments that vary based on the product and testing requirements.

Event Photography: Offer event photography services for parties, weddings, or corporate events. Earnings can vary widely based on event size, duration, and services offered. Rates may range from $100 to several hundred or more per hour.

TaskRabbit: Join platforms like TaskRabbit to offer various services to local clients. Rates vary based on the task but may range from $20 to $50 or more per hour for various services offered.

Remote Graphic Design: Provide graphic design services to clients online. Rates can vary widely based on project complexity and expertise, ranging from $50 to $150 or more per hour.

Remote Video Editing: Offer video editing services to content creators. Rates can range from $30 to $100 or more per hour, depending on the project's complexity and requirements.

Remote Bookkeeping: Help small businesses with their bookkeeping needs. Hourly rates may range from $20 to $50 or more, depending on the complexity of bookkeeping tasks and experience.

Healthcare Positions: If you're pursuing a healthcare degree, look for opportunities as a medical scribe or home health aide. Earnings vary based on the role, qualifications, and location. Medical scribes may earn hourly rates of $10 to $20 or more, while home health aides may earn $15 to $25 per hour or more.

Remote Research: Assist researchers and organizations with data collection and analysis. Compensation can vary widely based on the project and organization, ranging from hourly rates of $15 to $50 or more.

Online Language Translation: Offer language translation services for documents, websites, or videos. Rates vary based on language pairs and complexity, ranging from $0.05 to $0.30 or more per word.

Catering: Start a small catering business for events and parties. Earnings can vary widely based on the event size, menu, and services offered. Rates may range from a few hundred to several thousand dollars per event.

Cleaning Services: Offer deep cleaning or specialized cleaning services for local residents or businesses. Rates can vary based on the services provided and property size, typically ranging from $20 to $50 per hour.

Car Detailing: Provide car detailing services for those looking to keep their vehicles clean and well-maintained. Prices vary based on services offered, but typical rates can range from $50 to $150 or more for a complete car detailing service.

Freelance Writing and Editing: Write articles, blogs, or offer editing services to businesses and individuals. Rates can range from $0.01 to $0.10 or more per word for content creation or editing services. Writing can be more profitable than most people think.

Graphic Design for Local Businesses: Create logos, flyers, or marketing materials for local businesses. Rates can vary widely based on the project scope and expertise, ranging from $50 to $500 or more per project for logos, flyers, or marketing materials.

Test Prep Tutoring: Help students prepare for standardized tests like the SAT or GRE. Hourly rates often range from $20 to $100 or more, depending on the subject, level of expertise, and market demand.

Pet Grooming: If you have the skills and equipment, offer pet grooming services. Earnings can vary widely based on services offered and location, but grooming services often range from $30 to $100 or more per session.

Resume Writing: Help fellow students and job seekers craft effective resumes. Rates often range from $50 to $200 or more per resume, depending on experience and the level of customization.

Rent Out Your Parking Space: If you have an extra parking spot, rent it to fellow students or residents. Income can vary based on location and demand, potentially ranging from a few dollars per day to several hundred dollars per month.

Home Renovation or Repairs: Offer basic home renovation or repair services if you have the necessary skills. Earnings vary widely based on the project size and complexity, typically ranging from a few hundred to several thousand dollars per project.

Handmade Jewelry or Clothing: Create and sell handmade jewelry or clothing. Income varies based on product quality and marketing efforts, potentially ranging from a few dollars to hundreds per item sold.

Influencer Marketing: Build a social media following and collaborate with brands on sponsored posts. Income can vary significantly based on follower count and brand collaborations, potentially ranging from a few hundred to thousands of dollars per sponsored post or collaboration.

Remote Coding: Work as a remote coder, especially if you have expertise in programming languages. Rates can vary widely, but experienced coders can earn hourly rates ranging from $50 to $150 or more depending on the project complexity and expertise.

E-book Publishing: Write and publish e-books on platforms like Amazon Kindle. Earnings vary based on book sales, with potential income ranging from a few dollars to thousands per month.

Fitness Classes: Offer fitness classes or personal training sessions both in person and online. Income can vary based on class fees and client base, with potential earnings ranging from $20 to $100 or more per class or session.

Language Interpretation: Provide interpretation services for individuals or businesses. Hourly rates may range from $20 to $50 or more, depending on the language and industry.

Medical Transcription: Transcribe medical documents or records for healthcare providers. Rates can vary based on the volume and complexity of documents, potentially ranging from $15 to $30 or more per hour.

Podcast Hosting: Start and host your own podcast, monetizing it through sponsorships and ads. Income from sponsorships and ads can vary widely, but successful podcasts can earn from a few hundred to thousands of dollars per episode.

Online Gaming Tournaments: Compete in or organize online gaming tournaments for cash prizes. Earnings can vary greatly based on tournament entry fees, prizes, and organization, potentially ranging from small amounts to significant cash prizes.

Yard Sales and Flea Markets: Sell used or vintage items at yard sales or local flea markets. Income varies based on item sales and prices, potentially ranging from a few dollars to hundreds per event.

Virtual Event Hosting: Host online events or webinars on topics of interest. Income can vary, but hosts may charge fees ranging from $10 to $100 or more per attendee, depending on the event's value.

Writing for Content Mills: Write articles and content for content mills that pay per word. Rates often range from $0.01 to $0.10 or more per word, depending on the platform and content.

Photography Editing: Offer photo editing services for photographers. Rates vary based on the complexity of the editing, but they can range from $20 to $100 or more per hour.

These income estimates are approximate and can fluctuate based on various factors, including location, expertise, market demand, and individual efforts put into marketing and networking. Individuals pursuing these income sources should research market rates and consider their own skills and circumstances when determining potential earnings.

Other ideas:

Spend $xxx on a huge pallet of Amazon returns, and see what you can sell the items for locally and/or online.

Spend $800 on a huge haul of lost luxury cargo, and see what you can sell the items for locally and/or online.

Buy some lost mail packages for re-sale.

Buy some lost TEMU packages (for cheap) for re-sale.

Buy some lost Nordstrom returns (for cheap) for re-sale.

Disclaimer: Please be aware none of this information constitutes financial advice or recommendations. Readers should do their own research before taking any actions related to these ideas and statements.

Chapter 10: The AI Revolution

The mind, once stretched by a new idea,

never returns to its original dimensions.

— Ralph Waldo Emerson

Emerson's words ring more accurate than ever for Gen Z, as the new idea is artificial intelligence (AI). AI isn't just a buzzword; it's the engine driving the future, and YOU are positioned perfectly to take the wheel. The exciting part? You don't have to wait until after college to participate in this revolution—you can dive in now.

For many, this idea is just a couple of years old. Artificial intelligence is a lot older than that. However, the purpose of this chapter is not to go over the long history of AI. Instead, it is about how you can participate in The AI Revolution.

Students, there are Idea$, and then there are AI ideas.

Whereas the previous chapter was about getting to work with a choice of jobs from our long list. This chapter isn't about manual labor. Instead, it is mostly about computer labor. Namely, the power of computers. Large language models (LLMs), specifically.

The previous chapter was admittedly "old school," whereas this chapter is decidedly new school (even new world). It is dedicated to seeking the potential in an unknown frontier.

Changing the World

Many high school and college students are ditching the classroom to join: The AI Revolution. This movement can be joined while you are in high school, college, and beyond college. It is an equal opportunity employer (without, at times, a W-2 job necessary). It's a revolution reshaping how we live, work, and learn. And it's Gen Z's opportunity to participate and thrive.

It is being called the AI gold rush, the AI tsunami. A tidal wave of machine learning paired with the unbound potential of the human mind. Limitless potential, any creation or task is possible now to anyone willing to sit down and learn to tell it what to do.

TechCruch says that OpenAI has become "one of the most-hyped companies in recent memory." OpenAI says its mission is to ensure that artificial general intelligence benefits all of humanity. We will see.

You may, however, have read articles dismissing this revolution and calling it the "AI Bubble" (as the shares of Nvidia stock continue to rise). No worries. Plenty of folks underestimate tech revolutions like AI, often to their downfall.

Stanford professor Andrew Ng calls AI "the new electricity."

OpenAI CFO Sarah Friar says artificial intelligence isn't experimental anymore. She says banks, financial institutions, and fintech's are using it daily in their businesses.

This is the mentality you need to join the AI Revolution. Just like electricity transformed industries in the past, AI will change how we live, work, and dream.

AI is also the current sea change in automation.

Creative Destruction

If you want to sound like an economic genius to others, consider looking up the term "creative destruction" identified by economist Joseph Schumpeter a century ago. It describes how new innovations replace and make older goods and services obsolete. It "never can be stationary" said the economist. The focus will always be on new markets and new methods of production.

Creative destruction is such a challenging concept that it is rarely introduced and discussed, even in foundational courses in undergraduate economics. This is another example of why this social science is often called the "dismal science." Economics professors would instead present the rudiments of subjects such as fiscal and monetary policy. Gen Z need needs not be concerned with old-school economics; rather, it needs to concentrate on the new world of AI economics.

Creative destruction has always happened in places like Silicon Valley year after year.

Examples of disruptive technology over time include the printing press, the cotton gin, the radio, automobiles, airplanes, the film industry, CDs, computers, the Internet, Napster, iPhone, and the Apple Store.

And now we have AI, artificial intelligence. AI has been with us for a while, but never like this.

What do members of Gen Z need to do? First, take a deep breath and calm the nerves. Leaping into the unknown, fearing it might not work out, will only complicate things. Don't think about why it won't; think about why it will, and even if it doesn't work out, you're just back where you are now. In the words of the great Toni Morrison, "If you want to fly, give up everything that weighs you down!"

Retrain and reinvent yourself based on what you like to do.

We see that AI is enabling the automation of labor that isn't just manual and routine but also cognitive and non-routine. So there will be job losses in some industries, especially for some people later in their careers who won't be able to successfully pivot in this new environment.

"Everyone who works in an information industry — a category that includes journalists, software coders, and stock pickers — should be thinking about whether, or perhaps when, a computer is going to take their job," said a senior editor of the Financial Times. This is a clear message about job losses in certain sectors.

However, in the medium and long term, you are and will be seeing some dynamic growth opportunities. The AI marketplace is truly a trillion-dollar opportunity. Are you interested? Are you a player?

It has already been taking place in early-stage startups and elsewhere. In this ecosystem, these new companies use AI to automate or make a specific work or process function more efficient. It is all about a reallocation of capital. Again, symptoms of creative destruction.

But this AI world is not just about startups.

OpenAI CEO Sam Altman said, "The thing I'm most worried about right now is, the sort of, the speed and magnitude of the socioeconomic change may have, and what the impacts on what that will be."

So, again, the question becomes: Gen Z, do you want in? The AI revolution is in full swing, and it's time to decide: Will you be a spectator watching as those around you succeed? Or will you be a player willing to risk failure for personal goals of success? In the words of Gen Z, "Will you be the CEO?"

Gen Z Stories

You don't need to drop out of school to join the AI movement. But many have abandoned PLAN A to join the revolution. The AI entrepreneurs noted below did, and there are dozens of other examples.

Govind Gnanakumar, the cofounder of Automorphic, was "surprised by the slow pace of learning" in his computer science courses. So, he quit Georgia Tech in 2022 with his other student partners. He was then accepted into the prestigious Y Combinator program to launch his AI startup.

Jay Dang, 21, withdrew from the University of California, Berkeley, to establish FlowGPT, a generative AI applications company. Dang views this decision as the best he's ever made. FlowGPT reports a substantial user base and a valuation of $12 million after raising $2 million in seed money.

These startups are not rare success stories but part of a fast-growing trend. The message is clear: AI is the new gold rush. Gen Z, many of your peers have already stepped up. You are uniquely positioned to excel in AI.

AI Is Empowering YOU

The good news is this. You can join the AI Revolution and put any of your educational plans in action: PLAN A, B, C, or D. You can join the revolution full-time or part-time.

AI gives every student a 1-on-1 tutor.

Some are calling AI an economic AI tsunami. Some are worried about AI, calling it dangerous, and have expressed anxiety and fears. It is disruptive, no doubt. The authors of this book are enthusiastic about AI's possibilities.

Some have said that AI is akin to introducing the Guttenberg printing press.

For further information, read American computer scientist Ray Kurzweil about The Singularity. He is optimistic about civilization achieving new heights of intelligence, material progress, and longevity.

Yes, the speed and scale of ChatGPT and other LLMs are real. AI will be the printing press of this unprecedented new era of humanity. The question remains: How will you answer the call?

Join or Form a Hacker House

Many college students are not waiting around for an introductory undergraduate class in AI to learn about the subject's essentials. They are diving into AI themselves or with others.

How are some in Gen Z learning and doing AI? Some, while in college, form or join a hacker house.

A hacker house? What is that?

Our Appendix H describes hacker houses as collaborative living spaces where like-minded individuals—students, tech enthusiasts, and entrepreneurs—live and work together on cutting-edge projects.

Students are using AI as a supplement to their college education. They are working on AI projects for companies and also forming startups.

Pretty cool. Yes?

What are some of the things these AI hackers do? They build things to solve problems and add value to products.

1. AI-Powered Chatbots and Apps for Businesses

2. Blockchain-Based Voting System

3. AI-Driven Personal Finance Management App

4. Autonomous Drone Delivery System

5. Decentralized Cloud Storage Solution

6. Wearable Health Monitoring Devices

7. Smart Campus Infrastructure

8. AI-Enhanced Educational Platform

9. Virtual Reality (VR) for Remote Collaboration

10. Cybersecurity Threat Detection Software

These projects align with current tech trends and provide valuable hands-on experience with advanced technologies such as AI, blockchain, IoT (Internet of Things), and cybersecurity, positioning hacker house residents to push boundaries and innovate.

We are attempting to stimulate your frontal lobes. These lobes allow us to think creatively and develop new solutions, specifically for problem-solving purposes.

[Students, many hacker houses require interviews and a demonstrated skill set. One computer science course and a WordPress site may not be enough to gain admission to many houses. No matter, form your own house instead.]

Hacker houses do not focus exclusively on AI. Other projects involving AWS (Amazon Web Services), blockchain, and Web 3 are worked on.

You won't find hacker houses mentioned in any pre-pandemic college guides you may consult.

There are hacker houses worldwide, from Hong Kong to Puerto Rico and Bangalore. The exact number of college hacker houses in the San Francisco Bay Area isn't readily available, but best estimates suggest several dozen. Many well-known ones exist, such as Hack Reactor, Hackbright Academy, HackHer, and General Assembly.

The Future of Jobs

Contrary to fears about AI eliminating jobs, it's creating new roles and redefining what work looks like. The job title "prompt engineer" didn't even exist a few years ago, yet now prompt engineers earn anywhere between $75,000 and $370,000 annually. These are careers that leverage AI to shape industries, solve complex problems, and design the future.

In this evolving landscape, it's not about AI replacing you—it's about how you can use AI to succeed. As one expert put it: "AI won't replace you. But a person using AI will."

Do all of these prompt engineers have college degrees from fancy, brand-name universities? Of course not.

Prompt Engineer Annual Income ($ USD) 2024

$175,000 - $335,000 Bloomberg

$250,000 - $335,000 Anthropic AI

$76,000 - $113,000 FutureWork

$200,000 - $370,000 OpenAI Prompt Engineer

$73,000 - $438,000 ZipRecruiter

AI: A New Vocabulary

All specialized fields in technology have their own set of concepts and vocabulary terms, and AI is no different.

How many AI terms do you know?

Artificial Intelligence (AI)

Machine Learning

Deep Learning

Data Mining

Speech Recognition

Chatbots

Natural Language Processing

Computer Vision

Google AI: Free Courses

Here are many free AI courses offered by Google that you can, and probably should, take advantage of online:

Google AI Essentials: This course covers the basics of AI, including how to use generative AI tools to boost productivity and enhance your work. It includes hands-on activities, assessments, and resources, and you can earn a certificate upon completion.

Machine Learning & AI Courses on Google Cloud: These courses cover topics from beginner to advanced levels, including Vertex AI, BigQuery, TensorFlow, Cloud Vision, and Natural Language API. They are designed to help you prepare for roles like Data Scientist, Machine Learning Engineer, or Contact Center Engineer.

12 Days of No-Cost Generative AI Training: This free series of on-demand courses, labs, and videos. It covers various aspects of generative AI and is designed to help you validate your AI skills.

These courses provide an excellent opportunity to learn AI skills from experts at Google. Which one are you most interested in?

Next Step

So, if you decide to join the AI Revolution in some capacity after graduating high school, you are electing to do so under any of the available plan strategies: PLAN A, B, C, or D.

Our recommendation for students in high school (and beyond) is to begin taking advantage of many free online AI courses as soon and as frequently as possible. Courses are being made available by Microsoft, Google, Nvidia, IBM, MIT, and others. Stack skills, certificates, and knowledge. You can be certified with Machine Learning certificates before you graduate high school.

While there is always a risk to joining a revolution and embracing entrepreneurship, this risk can be seen as minimized due to the size of the opportunity and the AI marketplace. Jay Dang left the University of California Berkeley to co-found FlowGPT, a generative AI applications company, for models like Google's Gemini and

Anthropic's Claude. Dang calls this decision the best he's ever made and has raised $10 million from venture capital investors.

The good news, we suppose, is that there would be a "PLAN B" available to your original PLAN B if your AI venture or career does not work out. Also, you can always go back to college if you fail.

AI is not just some new tech tool—we know it's a revolution. Gen Z was born at the perfect time to join and lead it. So, what will you do? Will you build the next billion-dollar AI startup? Will you use AI to solve problems in healthcare, education, or the environment? The possibilities are endless, and it starts with your decision today.

This book does not recommend that you buy our course (we don't have one), join a Discord channel for $29 a month, or do something similar. We recommend opening your mind to the challenges and opportunities before you. Sure, it may be overwhelming at times, but be grateful for that.

Developing your skill set, relationships, and resources needs to be done. It will involve hard work. If your future requires AI, great, so be it. Suppose it means something else; that would be great as well. Gen Z, open up your mind and do something!

Gen Z, you were born at the perfect time for the AI Revolution. It is yours to take. Step into it and shape the future.

Chapter 11: Gen Z Entrepreneur

Gen Z, this is your time. Entrepreneurship is an opportunity to consider no matter your academic status. Entrepreneurship is the ultimate freedom, the ultimate goal a person can dream of. And you can have it all. The tides have changed, the wind has blown. Business is no longer a brick-and-mortar shop selling tangible goods. It is a game of attention now. It's not just a matter of selling products; it's a matter of influencing people to buy from you.

The Creator Economy

The creator economy has undoubtedly exploded on social media over the past several years.

The first creator to reach 100 million followers is the social media personality and dancer Charli D'amelio (@charlidamelio), who is 20. She now has 155 million followers.

Charli quickly rose to prominence on TikTok by posting dance videos. She starred in a Hulu reality series and won "Dancing with the Stars" in 2022.Charli has launched various business ventures, including a nail polish collection, makeup, and clothing line.

No, Charli has not attended college, but she doesn't have to since The New York Times calls her the "reigning queen" of TikTok. Her estimated net worth is $30 million.

The creator economy is not just very big; it is huge. Charli D'amelio is just one example. Sure, she is a prominent and exceptional example, but shows us what is possible.

Markiplier and PewDiePie are two of the most successful and influential YouTubers, especially among Gen Z. Their impact on the creator space is profound, and they have both carved out unique niches that have garnered massive followings.

Markiplier's Success

Markiplier (@Markiplier), whose real name is Mark Fischbach, started his YouTube journey in 2012. His Let's Play videos quickly gained popularity, particularly in the horror genre. His energetic commentary and genuine reactions have captivated millions, and he now boasts over 37 million subscribers. Markiplier has expanded his brand beyond gaming, venturing into podcasts, live tours, and a clothing line. His success has earned him numerous awards, including four Streamy Awards and a Golden Joystick Award.

PewDiePie's Success

PewDiePie (@PewDiePie), whose real name is Felix Kjellberg, began his YouTube career in 2010. Known for his Let's Play videos, vlogs, and comedy shorts, PewDiePie has amassed over 110 million subscribers and 29.4 billion views. His humorous commentary and relatable content have made him one of the most popular creators on the platform. PewDiePie has also been recognized with several awards, including a Kids' Choice Award and multiple Streamy Awards.

Consider social media as one of your options to make an income or to make a living. Are you going to keep being a social media consumer, or will you take action and be a producer or creator? Social media is not going away anytime soon. There are over 2 billion active monthly users on Instagram. This is one of the reasons that $META stock has tripled over the past couple of years.

Gen Z and the creator economy. A perfect match.

WE believe in YOU.

Old School Startups

Learn from Successful College Startups

Many successful companies started as college projects. Learning from these examples can provide inspiration and valuable lessons for your entrepreneurial journey.

> Michael Dell founded Dell Technologies while he was a University of Texas at Austin student.

> Bill Gates and Paul Allen started Microsoft while Gates was a student at Harvard University.

> Mark Zuckerberg launched Facebook from his dorm room at Harvard University.

> Larry Page and Sergey Brin started Google as a research project while they were Ph.D. students at Stanford University.

Oh Canada!

In economics textbooks, the term barter is defined as an immediate reciprocal exchange of goods or services without using a medium of exchange (e.g. money).

Several decades ago, a blogger from British Columbia, over a series of 14 barter trades, was able to trade one red paperclip for a two-story farmhouse in Saskatchewan. He wrote a book and had a TED talk.

Yes, this is a somewhat dated example. Yet, it illustrates what is possible when entrepreneurs think creatively. If a random blogger can trade a singular paperclip all the way up to a two-story farmhouse, you can set up a business with a couple of people in a garage.

Building your brand and online profile

Do people know about you? Do you have a profile?

You probably have Instagram, TikTok, and Snapchat accounts.

But as you get closer to college, you must develop your brand. The professional you. Here's why:

Creating a LinkedIn profile during high school is a smart way to get ahead in planning for your future. While you might think LinkedIn is only for college graduates or professionals, it's also a fantastic tool for high school students, too! Through LinkedIn, you can network, find internships, research colleges, and explore potential career paths. When setting up your profile, include details about your education, part-time jobs, volunteer work, and leadership roles. A professional profile photo and headline that reflects your career goals will help others take notice of your potential.

One of the most significant advantages of LinkedIn is the ability to network. Connect with teachers, family members, or professionals in fields that interest you. Following colleges, companies, and scholarship organizations can keep you updated on exciting opportunities. By staying active and engaging authentically, you can showcase your accomplishments and make meaningful connections that could open doors in the future.

It's never too early to start thinking about your future! LinkedIn can help you research colleges and even connect with alumni for advice. Whether you're exploring career ideas or looking for internships, using LinkedIn to highlight your high school achievements can set you apart. So, start building your profile today, and don't be afraid to reach out for recommendations and advice—you'll take your first steps toward success!

To the Man (and Woman) in the Arena:

It is not the critic who counts: not the man who points out how the strong man stumbles or where the doer of deeds could have done better. The credit belongs to the man who is actually in the arena, whose face is marred by dust and sweat and blood, who strives valiantly, who errs and comes up short again and again, because there is no effort without error or shortcoming, but who knows the great enthusiasms, the great devotions, who spends himself in a worthy cause; who, at the best, knows, in the end, the triumph of high achievement, and who, at the worst, if he fails, at least he fails while daring greatly, so that his place shall never be with those cold and timid souls who knew neither victory nor defeat.

—Theodore Roosevelt

Speech at the Sorbonne, Paris, April 23, 1910

Show Me The Money

For many years, college athletes have cried, "Show Me The Money" (Jerry Maguire, 1996). Now, some of them have finally have achieved this. This is the game-changing NIL opportunity for college athletes that is now available.

For decades, college athletes were defined by a simple but challenging title: student-athletes. Their mission was to juggle the intense demands of their sport with an academic workload. Today, the landscape has shifted dramatically, and athletes are no longer just balancing education and competition—they're becoming entrepreneurs. Thanks to the introduction of NIL (Name, Image, and Likeness) rights, college athletes now have unprecedented opportunities to earn money while still in school, opening up a world of potential beyond the playing field. The NIL train has left the station and the college sports world is moving ahead at a breakneck pace.

The NIL Revolution: What's Changed?

In 2021, the NCAA made a historic decision, allowing college athletes to profit from their name, image, and likeness. No longer are athletes restricted from earning income, and this change has transformed the way student-athletes approach both their sports and their futures.

Today, athletes can sign endorsement deals, get paid for social media posts, make money from appearances, and explore various commercial opportunities. This change has ushered in a new era of sports marketing and financial independence for athletes who now have a platform to leverage their talents in more ways than ever before. College athletics is now the minor league or sports farm teams for the pros.

Not all athletes earn money, however. On an average Division I college football team, around 50-60% of players are involved in NIL deals.

Top Earners Leading the Way

There are college quarterbacks earning $1-4 million dollars annually. Along with top basketball stars earning $3-4 million. There names are well known. (Mentioning their names here would be informational and part of the narrative. Yet, it is always best to be cautious and respectful of their rights).

Gatorade, Nike, State Farm, Dr. Pepper, and Body Armor are some of the heavy-hitting brands that are partnering with athletes to promote their products.

Before NIL reached high schools, some of these athletes had quite large social media accounts, and they were not getting paid for them because it was illegal to do so. Many of these athletes felt cheated and pushed for the right to profit from their own likeness.

The popularity of these players has reached the point that the University of Tennessee announced it is adding a 10% "talent fee" to its football tickets. The money will be used to pay $22 million in player salaries starting in 2025.

Lessons for College Athletes: Maximizing NIL Potential

So, what can current and future college athletes learn from this? Here's how you can take full advantage of the NIL environment:

Build Your Personal Brand Early: Your brand matters whether you're a star quarterback or a rising tennis player. Use social media to showcase your sports talents, personality, and interests. Companies want to partner with athletes who have a story to tell.

Think Like an Entrepreneur: The NIL market has turned college sports into a business. Get familiar with contracts, negotiations, and marketing strategies. You don't have to be a business major to profit from NIL, but a savvy mindset will take you far.

Partner with Trustworthy Brands: Your name and image are powerful assets. Make sure you're partnering with brands that align with your values and won't tarnish your reputation. Not all deals are good deals.

Learn Financial Literacy: With ample opportunities come significant responsibilities. Managing money, planning for taxes, and investing wisely are crucial skills. Now's the time to learn financial management, as some athletes earn life-changing sums while still in college.

Navigating the Challenges of NIL

While the success stories are inspiring, not every NIL journey goes smoothly. There are now several examples of unfulfilled verbal promises from some Division 1 NCAA programs, leading to frequent misunderstandings within the space.

These experiences serve as a cautionary tale: make sure your agreements are solid, documented, and transparent. You don't want to get caught up in a legal battle.

The legal arena surrounding NIL continues to test new legal theories. In 2024, several former University of Michigan football players launched a class action lawsuit against the NCAA and Big Ten Network, seeking more than $50 million for being "wrongfully and unlawfully denied" NIL money. (These players left school well before NIL existed)

Why NIL Matters for Your Future

The NIL environment isn't just about making money during college. It's about setting yourself up for future success. By taking control of your brand, developing entrepreneurial skills, and learning how to handle financial opportunities, you're laying the foundation for life after sports—whether that's in professional athletics, business, or another career.

The NIL era is full of potential, but it also demands that athletes step up, not just as competitors, but as smart, strategic professionals. The future of college sports is here, and with NIL, the power is in your hands.

Embrace this moment, grow your brand, and leverage every opportunity that comes your way. This is your chance to turn your college sports journey into something more significant than you ever imagined!

NIL in High School

While NIL changed the college sports landscape, it has quickly impacted high school athletes. Over the past several years, high school athletes have begun cashing in as well. As of this writing, around 40 states have new rules in place to allow high school student-athletes to enjoy the benefits of NIL without losing their eligibility. California was the first state to allow athletes to sign NIL deals. In 2024, The Florida High School Athletic Association unanimously approved student-athletes getting paid based on their NIL.

One sports director, in 2022, said "It's here and it's here much faster than we thought."

Monetization, money management, and brand management are now part of these athletes' vocabulary, allowing some top high-school athletes to earn six figures from endorsement deals.

One California attorney recently acknowledged the obvious, "It's getting bigger by the day."

Most parents are very positive about these new rules for their athletes. Many parents have invested considerable time and money in their child athletes in the hope of college scholarships. Now, they can help monetize their athletes while still in high school.

Critical Points for High School NIL:

State-by-State Rules: The landscape of NIL rights for high school athletes varies significantly from state to state. Some states have enacted laws explicitly permitting or restricting NIL activities for high school students, while others have adopted a more general approach. Be sure to check your state's specific regulations.

Eligibility Concerns: NIL deals can sometimes affect an athlete's eligibility to compete in high school sports. States may have rules to protect eligibility, but the guidelines can be complex.

Balance with Education: Schools stress that academics and athletics should remain the main focus. It's essential to ensure that NIL activities don't interfere with schoolwork or sports performance. These education goals have become more challenging.

Opportunities to Earn: High school athletes can earn money through social media, endorsements, and brand deals, but should be aware of any state restrictions, including age requirements.

School Policies: Some schools may have policies on how their logos, uniforms, or facilities can be used in NIL deals. Bylaws and guidelines will differ on a state by state basis. For example, in California, the governing body is the California Interscholastic Federation. (https://www.cifstate.org/governance/constitution/index)

Ethics and Integrity: Athletes must be careful about the deals they accept and ensure they don't compromise their academic or athletic standing.

Gen Z, families should consult their state's high school athletic association or a legal professional for detailed advice.

Top Gen Z high school athletes now tell their college recruiters, *"show me the NIL."* $$$

Chapter 12: Digital Nomads

Do you have a laptop, a smartphone, carry-on luggage, and a passport?

If so, you have some of the necessary pieces of equipment to become a digital nomad.

Yes, you need this basic equipment and also a lot of motivation to become to become a digital nomad. Planning, a strategy, financing, and a realistic understanding of the dynamics of this undertaking are also important.

Who Are Digital Nomads?

Imagine working from a beachside café in Bali, a cozy coffee shop in Lisbon, or a modern co-working space in Mexico City. Online videos and blog posts suggest that digital nomads are the cool kids who work a couple of hours a day, and travel to exotic locations around the world. Realistically, it is a lot more involved than that but that is imagery that is portrayed.

A digital nomad earns a living by working online while traveling to different locations. They often work from many different places relying on internet connectivity to perform their jobs. With Wi-Fi and additional tech tools, geographical borders have been erased, making it easier than ever before to adopt this lifestyle.

And Gen Z? You're made for this lifestyle! Your generations has already mastered remote tech tools that allow you to thrive in this fast-paced, connected world. You were born into this world. In 2024, about 18.1 million American workers identified as digital nomads, reflecting a significant increase over the past few years. This lifestyle appeals to those seeking flexibility, adventure, and the ability to explore new cultures while maintaining their careers.

Gen Z, along with Millennials, makes up a large portion of digital nomads; 26% of digital nomads are from Gen Z. This is the generation which values experiences over material possessions and is highly adaptable to remote work, making the digital nomad lifestyle particularly attractive.

Gen Z Americans are flocking to various countries that offer a mix of good internet connectivity, affordable living, and vibrant cultures. Some of the most popular destinations include: The United Kingdom, Canada, Japan, Netherlands, Singapore, Australia, Switzerland, Italy, Germany, and Ireland. These countries are the traditionally popular locations for digital nomads. They are generally favored for their quality of life, social programs, and the opportunity to experience diverse cultures.

Plan B begins

For many students, Plan A ideally involves going to college, selecting a good major, graduating with (hopefully) ZERO college debt, getting a good job, and beginning your career doing what you love and what you were trained to do.

But Plan B—the digital nomad route—gives you an alternative. Instead of diving into the educational world of high tuition and student loans, you could take that tuition money, save it, and travel the world while building your career online. It's not just about "seeing the world." It's about creating a life that lets you work and explore.

There are over 2 million members in the r/digitalnomad subreddit. Read some of these unfiltered opinions and form your own rather than accepting those of previous generations.

Why spend thousands on college when you could invest in yourself and real-world experiences? This plan isn't just about dropping out – it's dropping into a global classroom! A classroom you engineer and subscribe to.

"The world awaits you." (Paulo Coelho) We know that the world is continually getting more and more connected. This is especially true after the pandemic which has enabled the digital nomad lifestyle for many more people.

As a digital nomad, your Plan B needs planning and a strategy. It is more than just viewing a handful of YouTube videos and getting your passport ready to be stamped.

Next, you need a country to go to. A number of popular countries were previously noted. Below are the countries that are considered the new hotspots for Gen Z and digital nomads.

Exciting Emerging Hotspots:

>   Mexico (vibrant culture + great internet)

>   Thailand (amazing food + affordable living)

>   Portugal (perfect blend of old and new)

>   Vietnam (rapidly growing tech scene)

>   Georgia (emerging digital hub)

Countries like Mexico, Thailand, and Portugal are hotspots for digital nomads because they offer affordable living, fast Internet, and an incredible lifestyle. And the best part? The cost of living in many of these places is much cheaper than what you'd expect in the U.S., so you can live very well without breaking the bank.

Costa Rica offers a two-year residency with no investment and no taxes on foreign income, making it a top tax haven in Central America. Remote workers just need to show an income of $2,500 a month.

Bali, an island in western Indonesia, is well know for its digital nomad community. Yet, according to some, Bali has lost its appeal recently. For many digital nomads, the hotpots will dictated by places that can offer reliable, fast Internet and affordable rent prices.

Where do you stay? You can stay in an apartment, a series of rotating Airbnbs, in a work hostel, an RV, a boat, co-living rooms or spaces.

Wow. Cool. Interesting. Digital Nomads. Welcome to the digital nomad lifestyle. It sounds adventurous, romantic and exciting. Right? Well, maybe. You'll need a plan. Don't underestimate actively engaged in research and planning in your endeavor.

Real Talk: Challenges to Consider

Life as a digital nomad sounds like a dream, but it's not all smooth sailing. It isn't all Instagram photos and beach workdays. You want to have realistic expectations so that the plan you put into place has a high chance of success.

These are some issues to prepare for:

>   Initial adjustment period

>   Managing work-life balance

Building lasting relationships

Maintaining professional growth

Handling paperwork and visas

Personal financial management

Finding reliable Internet

Gen Z DNs report several drawbacks, such as: personal loneliness, the lack of community, and feeling isolated, and missing family and hometown friends. Homesickness is very real for some. Relationships you make are often on a surface level since people are always moving around. Some feel more homeless than being a digital nomad. After a while, some get a feeling they need a home base.

Lack of developing a professional network may impact your future career advancement and earnings, causing your career to stagnate. For example, the time you spend in Thailand may end up being much more expensive than you anticipated.

Growing a business in a country where you are not fluent in the language is not easy. There is nothing easy about growing a business, period.

At times, the digital nomad lifestyle isn't as unique as it once seemed. Country hopping and working a few hours a day or when you want can get challenging, especially when there are money concerns. This is the time to get refocused on work.

There can also be never-ending paperwork. It won't be an issue if you're only making short trips to different countries But once you start to settle 3 months, or 6 months or longer (in some countries) you have to figure out visas, residencies, paperwork and taxes - it's a lot to manage.

If you unfortunately find yourself in country with unreliable internet, you may need to spend a lot of money to upgrade to get a reliable connection.

Your skill set and background may limit your job opportunities. Computer programmers usually don't get remote jobs.

Be cautious about Digital Nomad Life Coaches. Most of these individuals lack real professional training (e.g. Psy D, LPC, LCPC, MD etc.) or authentic life experiences to be doing this sort of thing. In fact, many life coaches make most of their money by selling courses on how to become Life Coaches.

Regardless of the drawbacks, becoming a digital nomad will change your perspective. Taking a chance on this lifestyle may just well be worth it. Whether you want to embrace this personal change becomes a big question.

Gen Z, do your research and be realistic.

The Money

Ah, yes, the money. Many of these nomads make 2-5k a month, in dollars or euros, and if you think 2k is small, you're right, but the cost of living in many of these remote locations is dirt cheap, as they say.

Exciting digital nomad opportunities include:

Social media management

Content creation

Web design

Digital Marketing

AI/tech consulting

Virtual assistance

Translation services

Freelance writing

Photography/Videography

Get a Reliable Income Stream: Most digital nomads earn between $2,000 and $5,000 a month, which is plenty in many countries. Whether you're freelancing, doing remote work, or starting your own online business, focus on getting consistent work. Make a personal finance budget. Maybe you are not used to budgeting, but you need to understand and how to calculate what is coming in and going out. (aka cashflow)

Doing what? You can do many things and consider many services. Many opportunities are available. You can work for an agency, produce Facebook ads and leads for clients, produce videos, be a web designer, be a YouTuber, blogging, AI, sustainability, graphic designer, freelance photographer, create Snaps on Snapchat, be an influencer, a content creator, a virtual assistant, a translator.

A skill set is required for all of these positions, and that involves learning and research. Your personal skill set produces your income.

Build and develop your skills through online courses. If you offer services for work, create your profile on freelancing platforms like Upwork and Fiverr. Get set up in advance to be paid with PayPal or Square.

You need to network. Reach out to people on social media. Talk to people about your plans. Create a website. Be proactive.

Smart Planning for Success

Build your skills before you go

Save a safety net ($10,000-$20,000 recommended)

Research visa requirements

Join digital nomad communities

Set up international payment systems

Create a realistic budget

Choose your first destination wisely

Top Countries with Freedom

The Heritage Foundation publishes an annual Index of Economic Freedom which ranks countries according to several metrics aggregated to produce the index.

The Index is mentioned here since Gen Z is known to value freedom and place it high on their must-have list.

The top five countries, according to the Index, are as follows:

Rank	Country	Score
1	Singapore	83.5
2	Switzerland	83
3	Ireland	82.6
4	Taiwan	80
5	Luxembourg	79.2

[Countries with scores between 100-80 are considered Free, with countries with scores between 79.9-70 are considered Mostly Free.]

The Heritage Foundation's Index of Economic Freedom states that, "Economic freedom is the fundamental right of every human to control his or her own labor and property." The foundation measures 12 categories of economic freedom.

The United States is currently ranked #25 on the Index with a score of 70.1, its lowest ranking to date. The U.S. has dropped from a high of fourth place in 1995. It has been experiencing a slow and steady slide in the country rankings over many years. Most recently this drop is due to the pandemic lockdowns and poor fiscal health.

For Gen Z understanding the Index is valuable as a comparative tool and to examine country trends. Economics, culture, and history are important for digital nomads to research and evaluate. For example, the country of Vietnam is viewed as a popular destination for digital nomads due to its recent economic growth. In addition to economic freedom, to evaluate a country like Vietnam, Gen Z is encouraged to research other country elements such as culture, attitude toward Americans, history and the impact of wars. A holistic study of countries is encouraged to provide a more complete picture to determine how well it fits with individual digital nomad aspirations.

Some economists have challenged the utility of the Index. One criticized its data measurement factors as a poor barometer of freedom, while another determined the index is not correlated with country economic growth (GDP).

Passport

Do you have a U.S. passport? If not, why not apply and get one as soon as you can so you are prepared?

https://travel.state.gov/content/travel/en/passports/
how-apply.html

Our recommendation is to select the Expedited Passport Service. Sure, it is an extra 60 bucks, but it is well worth it.

Consult Appendix I: Get a U.S. Passport, for further information.

The appendix provides the steps on how to obtain a U.S. passport, highlighting its importance for activities for digital nomads or for college students participating in a study abroad program. Appendix I outlines the process for both first-time applicants and renewals, including necessary forms (DS-11 for first-time and DS-82 for renewals), required documentation, passport photo guidelines, and fees. It also details how to expedite the process, if needed, emphasizing the importance of securing a passport well in advance of any international travel plans.

Ready for Takeoff

Get your passport now

Research digital nomad visas (40+ countries offer them!)

Join online communities

Start building your skills

Begin saving

Plan your first country destination

The Future is Yours!!!

The digital nomad lifestyle represents freedom, growth, and endless possibilities. While it comes with challenges, the rewards are incredible: cultural immersion, personal growth, and the opportunity to design your own life. Live on the beach. See the world.

Remember: Every successful digital nomad started precisely where you are right now. The only difference? They took that first step. Get out there and go do it.

Are you ready to write your own unique adventure? The world is waiting, Gen Z!

Chapter 13: 1995

Digital Age Blast Off!!!!

How about a brief trip down Memory Lane?

This chapter is about the year 1995 in the United States of America. We highlight these events as a brief history lesson about the world Gen Z'ers were born into. The digital age has shaped this generation's identity.

Yes, we know some of you may disagree with our Gen Z born-on-date of 1995, but we have social scientists, anthropologists, and other observers on our side. We have to start somewhere.

And yes we know you can find some article, influencer, institution or some college professor who has a different or better date than 1995. So what? Are they going to help you achieve a ZERO COLLEGE DEBT game plan? No, of course not. We are the people helping you do that.

Since Gen Z was surely born into this digital world, we will start by reviewing the big tech events of 1995. This generation is unique in that they have grown up with nothing but access to the Internet - "digital natives."

In addition, the year 1995 was a turning point for the whole Internet industry. A watershed year had passed. That year may have been the most formative one for the web, according to some. The birth of Web 1.0 was a thrilling moment for everyone in the nation, not just Silicon Valley.

1995 Online Events

Numerous noteworthy occurrences and advancements in 1995 had a profound impact on the expansion and development of the Internet and the World Wide Web. Here are a few of the most important things that happened:

1. Windows 95 and Internet Explorer: Microsoft released Windows 95, a major operating system update that included built-in support for dial-up networking and introduced many people to the Internet for the first time. Alongside Windows 95, Microsoft launched Internet Explorer 1.0, marking its entry into the web browser market.

2. Launch of eBay and Amazon: eBay, an online auction platform, was founded by Pierre Omidyar in September 1995, allowing users to buy and sell goods online. Amazon.com, founded by Jeff Bezos, started as an online bookstore and quickly expanded into a variety of products.

3. The birth of JavaScript: Brendan Eich developed JavaScript in 1995, which became a crucial programming language for creating interactive web pages and applications.

4. AltaVista Search Engine: Digital Equipment Corporation launched AltaVista, one of the earliest and most powerful search engines at the time. It gained popularity for its advanced search capabilities.

5. Internet milestones: The Internet Engineering Task Force (IETF) released HTTP/1.0 as an official Internet protocol, which significantly contributed to the development of the web.

6. RealAudio and RealVideo: RealNetworks introduced RealAudio and RealVideo, making it possible for users to stream audio and video content over the Internet, paving the way for the multimedia streaming era.

7. Netscape IPO: Netscape Communications Corporation, known for its web browser Netscape Navigator, had a highly successful initial public offering (IPO), marking one of the early successes of Internet-related companies.

8. Web growth and user base: The number of websites continued to increase, and more people started accessing the Internet regularly. Email and web browsing became increasingly popular among the general public.

These events and advancements in 1995 played a crucial role in shaping the Internet and the World Wide Web, laying the foundation for the digital landscape that has continued to evolve and expand since then.

1995 Offline Events

Many interesting non-digital events occurred in 1995, such as:

> O.J. Simpson trial verdict (October 3, 1995)

> The Dayton Peace Agreement (November 21, 1995)

> and, two U.S. federal government shutdowns

In sports, The San Francisco 49ers won the Super Bowl, the Houston Rockets won the NBA Championship, the Atlanta Braves won the World Series in baseball, and the New Jersey Devils clinched the Stanley Cup in hockey.

FWIW

Microsoft released the Windows 95 operating system in 1995. Mick Jagger belted out the lyrics as part of Microsoft's Start Me Up campaign to promote Windows 95. Despite the OS's shortcomings (memory, hard disk limitations, and numerous other concerns), the advertisements were deemed pretty cool for its time. It cost Microsoft $3 million to license the Rolling Stones song.

Epilogue

So, if Gen Z'ers were born at the beginning of the Digital Age, then they should continue to embrace all things digital such as blockchain, generative AI, and crypto, correct? After all the average Gen Z'er engages in technology for over 10 hours each day.

Recently, TechCrunch reported that Amazon says it'll spend $230 million on generative AI startups. That is just the tip of the AI iceberg.

Chapter 14: Starbucks

Without further ado, in Chapter One, our "Straight Up" chapter, we outline several options or choices students have regarding their college decision.

With each of these options, of course, there are associated costs, risks, time factors, and benefits. And, with each of these elements individual student goals, dreams, and objectives need to be considered and customized.

With our "Plan D: The Starbucks solution," here we have a corporation completely covering your tuition. Yes, you read that correctly, 100% of your upfront tuition is covered. All that is necessary is employment with Starbucks. No doubt, zero tuition costs is an absolutely a huge benefit. Yes, other costs such as room, board and books need to be paid for. Sure, there is some significant expense there. Yet, since you are working for Starbucks and you are also getting a reliable and regular paycheck, this means you can do it without incurring any student loan debt! That should always remain one your principal college financial goals.

In reading this chapter further, you'll notice that well over 10,000 Starbucks partners have graduated from the program. No small thing, indeed. Starbucks is ready for you to brew some rocket fuel for their customers. Are you?

We selected Starbucks to highlight the details of their program. There are many other corporations which provide full or partial tuition assistance. Companies such as T-Mobile, Discover, Chipotle and others provide full tuition. Do your own research, since these programs can change over time.

If you are focused and serious about graduating with a respected college degree with NO COLLEGE DEBT; working and taking classes for college credit is an outstanding option, plus a smart decision.

Enjoy your Caffè Mocha

Ok, begin to enjoy your Caffè Mocha, or your Iced Caramel Macchiato, or your Salted Caramel Cream Cold Brew and let's brew up some college dreams with Starbucks and their SCAP program.

Here's everything you need to know about the program and its relationship with Arizona State University (ASU):

> The Starbucks College Achievement Plan (SCAP) is a first-of-its-kind partnership between Starbucks and Arizona State University (ASU) that provides eligible Starbucks partners (employees) with 100% upfront tuition coverage for a first-time bachelor's degree through ASU Online. It is designed to help Starbucks employees pursue higher education and earn a college degree with minimal financial burden.

Eligibility:

To be eligible for SCAP, you must be an active Starbucks employee (both part-time and full-time) in the United States. This includes baristas, shift supervisors, and other positions.

You need to work a minimum number of hours per week to qualify for the program.

Additional eligibility criteria include:

> Must not have a bachelor's degree.

Must complete the Free Application for Federal Student Aid (FAFSA).

Must have a complete financial aid file.

Must meet satisfactory academic progress (SAP).

Pathway to Admission:

If you do not meet the admission criteria for ASU, you may be eligible for the Pathway to Admission program. This program allows you to take up to 10 college-level courses to earn your admission into the university, with credit conversion costs fully covered.

Degree Options:

SCAP primarily offers undergraduate degree programs. However, it also provides support for select graduate programs in partnership with ASU.

Partnership with Arizona State University (ASU):

The Starbucks College Achievement Plan is a partnership between Starbucks and Arizona State University. ASU is the exclusive academic partner for SCAP. ASU is a leading public research university with over 110,000 students enrolled in over 170 undergraduate and graduate degree programs. ASU Online is ASU's online learning platform, which offers over 140 undergraduate and graduate degree programs.

SCAP participants can choose from a wide range of degree programs offered by ASU, which includes various fields of study such as business, healthcare, social sciences, and more. ASU is a well-regarded public research university known for its high-quality online education and commitment to accessibility.

The Starbucks College Achievement Plan has been a success since its launch in 2014. Over 10,000 Starbucks partners have graduated from the program, and over 23,000 partners are currently enrolled in the program or Pathway to Admission.

Financial Coverage:

Starbucks covers a significant portion of the tuition costs for eligible partners. This includes full tuition coverage for all four years of a bachelor's degree program for most partners.

The program also includes a reimbursement model, meaning that Starbucks covers the upfront cost of tuition, and you may need to pay a small portion that is reimbursed at the end of the semester.

Academic Support:

SCAP participants receive dedicated academic advising and support services from both Starbucks and ASU. Advisors help partners with enrollment, course selection, and academic progress.

The program is designed to be flexible, allowing partners to study and work simultaneously.

Continued Employment:

While enrolled in SCAP, partners are expected to maintain their employment at Starbucks. After completing their degrees, they are encouraged to continue working at the company.

No Obligation to Stay:

Unlike some other tuition assistance programs, SCAP does not require partners to commit to staying with Starbucks for a set period after completing their degrees.

Applying and Enrollment:

To apply for SCAP, eligible partners can visit the program's website and follow the application process.

Once accepted, partners can enroll in ASU courses and start their educational journey.

The Starbucks College Achievement Plan is lauded for its commitment to providing educational opportunities to its employees, making higher education more accessible and affordable. It's a prime example of a corporate partnership with a reputable educational institution (ASU) to help employees pursue their academic goals while continuing to work. Keep in mind that specific program details and eligibility criteria may change over time, so it's advisable to visit the official SCAP website or contact Starbucks for the most up-to-date information.

Conclusion:

The Starbucks College Achievement Plan is a valuable opportunity for eligible Starbucks partners to earn a bachelor's degree at no upfront cost. The program is a partnership between Starbucks and Arizona State University, and it offers over 140 undergraduate degree programs to choose from. If you are a Starbucks partner and are interested in earning a bachelor's degree, you are encouraged you to learn more about the Starbucks College Achievement Plan.

https://starbucks.asu.edu/

Chapter 15: Useless Majors

Do an online search for useless majors or worst degrees for college students and you'll find many of these lousy majors on the list below.

To be honest, these majors/degree are not necessarily totally useless or worthless. But, relatively speaking, yes they are. For your time and money, they have been proven to be incredibly poor educational investments.

Take the majors library science and interdisciplinary studies, for example. These two majors are often at the top of most lists of useless college degrees. Why is that? Several factors. The job market is very poor for those degrees and the anticipated income is likewise poor. The demand for these degrees have declined a great deal over the past five to ten years. And lastly, the barriers to entry are low and the employment opportunities equally low as well. Sure, you may be able to get a job and scratch out a living, but it won't be much of a living.

In checking out the list below, some may disagree with several selections. And some may even say, I know of such-and-such person who majored in 'xyz', and they got a good job after graduation. That's the exception, rather than the rule. You might read articles from academics and journalists taking issue with the notion of 'useless degrees.' Don't bet your future on these articles and on rare exceptions. "Useless majors" is not a myth, unfortunately it is a reality. Actual wages in the labor market determine this reality.

Also, for example, you might ask why is 'Advertising' is on the list? It is a business subject and business majors are in demand, right? Wrong (not all of them). Advertising is too general a subject to select as a major in and much too old-school. In class you'll study how to advertise Corn Flakes cereal (and other uninteresting brands) to demographics you could care less about. There is an old tale in the advertising business which goes like this: a business person says "I know 50% of my advertising budget is wasted, I just don't know which 50%!" Advertising used to be able get you a job with a cereal company or with a company selling soap detergent. Just try getting a job with a bland, uninspiring major like advertising today. Good luck, you'll need it. Companies today want majors in digital marketing, data science, cybersecurity or specialists in social media.

An editor from a major financial newspaper recently stated: "Everyone who works in an information industry — a category that includes journalists, software coders and stock pickers — should be thinking about whether, or perhaps when, a computer is going to take their job." This was a comment about the impact of AI across the current labor market. Research your major thoroughly! The consequences of going with PLAN A (plus, your original major selection) without doing your research can be quite costly.

Again, these majors may not be totally worthless, in some sense, but try making a decent living off them. We don't want our Gen Z readers and students to fall into the trap of thinking it won't happen to them.

Regretfully, our twenty-something recent graduate and friend Em, ("Reflections from Em") selected one of these majors and is now living with the financial consequences.

So, here is our list of Useless Majors, unranked and in no particular order:

Physical Fitness And Parks Recreation

Film, Video And Photographic Arts

Advertising

Fine arts

Theatrical Arts

Art History

Linguistic Studies

Philosophy

Religious Studies

Environmental Science

Astronomy

Music

Commercial Art And Graphic Design

English Language And Literature

Library Science

Humanities

Fashion Designing

Interdisciplinary Studies

Education

Astronomy

History

Public Relations

Management

Project Management

International Relations

Paralegal Studies

Anthropology

Archeology

Communications

Creative Writing

Criminal Justice

Culinary Arts

Biology

Physics

Psychology

Quiz time: Do you really want to be chained to a 20 or 30 or $40,000 student loan over the next ten years for one of these useless majors with no, poor or limited job prospects in that field?

Don't waste your time with these majors. There are much, much better options available for you, if you are serious about a good career, life, and GRADUATING FROM COLLEGE DEBT FREE!

Permit us to point out the obvious. If you find yourself in one of those unfortunate majors on this list, consider changing. There is probably enough time to do so. You may be interested in a major's subject area and it may be your current passion. But, if it will not deliver with a return on your invested time and money, you'll end up frustrated and in debt. The time to be realistic about college choice is now, rather than later.

Understanding the importance of aligning your degree with current labor market demand in your specialty.

Some Fun Quotes

All in the spirit of good fun and humor, here are several quotes from college students characterizing their majors. Specifically stereotypes or what others think or red flags about their chosen major.

"we think we're smarter than every one else but we're really not"

Neurobiology major

"we make TikToks for class"

Marketing major

"we don't know how to do maths or something"

Dance major

"we don't shower"

Computer Science major

"all we care about is money"

Finance major

"we don't really do anything and we picked the major because it is easy"

Communications major

"all of us want to be lawyers"

Political Science

"we're just big nerds"

Biology major

Identifying degrees with strong job prospects

Not all degrees offer the same return on investment. This is one of the main (obvious) points in this chapter.

Gen Z students need to avoid fields with limited career opportunities. Otherwise a life of career frustration and limited choices typically follow after college graduation.

Choosing a major/degree with strong job prospects is crucial for ensuring that your investment in education pays off. Make your education relevant. Think about the future and your future! Here are steps to help you identify degrees that are likely to lead to successful careers.

Research Labor Market Trends:

Utilize resources such as the U.S. Bureau of Labor Statistics (BLS) Occupational Outlook Handbook to research job growth projections and average salaries for various professions.

Look for fields with above-average growth rates, indicating higher demand for professionals in those areas.

Consider STEM Fields:

Degrees in science, technology, engineering, and mathematics (STEM) are known for strong job prospects and high earning potential.

Examples include computer science, engineering, data science, and cybersecurity.

Healthcare and Allied Health Professions:

Healthcare is a rapidly growing field with numerous opportunities. Degrees in nursing, physical therapy, medical technology, and healthcare administration are in high demand.

The aging population and advancements in medical technology continue to drive growth in this sector.

Business and Finance:

Degrees in business administration, finance, and accounting often lead to stable and lucrative career paths.

Specializations such as management information systems (MIS) and supply chain management are also highly valued.

Emerging Technologies:

Consider fields related to emerging technologies, such as artificial intelligence, machine learning, renewable energy, and biotechnology.

These areas are expected to grow significantly as technology advances and society shifts towards more sustainable practices.

Avoiding Fields with Limited Career Opportunities

While pursuing your passion is important, it's equally crucial to be aware of fields with limited job prospects or lower earning potential. Here are some tips to help you avoid degrees that may not offer a strong return on investment.

Assess Employment Rates:

Research the employment rates for graduates in specific fields. Degrees with high unemployment rates may indicate limited job opportunities.

Utilize alumni data from colleges and universities to gauge the success of graduates in finding employment related to their degrees.

Evaluate Salary Potential:

Compare the average starting salaries for different degrees. Fields with low salary potential may not provide a sufficient return on the cost of education.

Websites such as Payscale and Glassdoor can provide salary insights for various professions.

Consider Industry Trends:

Be mindful of industries that are shrinking or being disrupted by technology. Degrees tied to declining industries may have limited future opportunities.

Stay informed about economic shifts and technological advancements that could impact job availability in certain fields.

Engage in Career Planning:

Start career planning early by exploring potential career paths and the education requirements for those careers.

Seek guidance from career counselors, academic advisors, and industry professionals to understand the demand for specific degrees.

Pursue Internships and Work Experience:

Gain practical experience through internships, co-op programs, and part-time jobs related to your field of study.

Real-world experience not only enhances your resume but also provides insight into the job market and helps you make informed decisions about your career.

Network with Industry Professionals:

Build a network of contacts in your desired industry through professional associations, LinkedIn, and industry events.

Networking can provide valuable information about job opportunities, industry trends, and the skills employers are looking for.

Stay Flexible and Adaptable:

The job market is constantly evolving, so it's important to stay flexible and adaptable.

Be open to continuous learning and professional development to keep your skills relevant and in demand.

Consider Alternative Credentials:

In addition to a degree, consider obtaining certifications, licenses, or other credentials that can enhance your employability.

Professional certifications in fields such as IT, healthcare, and finance can demonstrate specialized knowledge and skills to employers.

By carefully selecting a degree that aligns with market demand and offers strong job prospects, you can maximize the return on your educational investment and reduce the risk of incurring unnecessary debt. This proactive approach will set you on a path to a successful and financially stable career.

Top 5 Highest-Paying College Majors

FWIW, according to Payscale (September 2024), the following majors pay the best as measured by mid-career annual earnings:

1. Petroleum engineering $212,100

2. Operations research and industrial engineering $202,600

3. Electrical engineering and computer science $192,300

4. Interaction design $178,800

5. Building science $172,400

Chapter 16: The New FAFSA

Navigating the New FAFSA: Your Key to Financial Aid

It has arrived!

The updated FAFSA, which encountered some major technical difficulties during the rollout, is now available and can assist families and students in their pursuit of college financial aid.

Applying for federal student aid has never been easier than with the new Free Application for Federal Student Aid (FAFSA®). The application procedure has been simplified, and thanks to these updates, more people are now eligible for federal aid. Forbes calls the new FAFSA a major facelift and redesign.

Let's review

What is the FAFSA?

The Free Application for Federal Student Aid (FAFSA) is a form that students and their families complete to apply for Federal and State financial aid for college or graduate school. The FAFSA is your gateway to unlocking financial aid opportunities and reducing the burden of college costs. Understanding and navigating the FAFSA process is crucial for Gen Z students seeking to graduate debt-free.

If you hear that filling out the FAFSA is pointless, run the other way. Bad advice abounds. No, it's not pointless. You can lose tens of thousands of dollars in annual grants and scholarships.

It is more vital than ever to be well-prepared and act quickly to maximize FAFSA benefits since certain aid is provided on a first-come, first-served basis.

Go to studentaid.gov to fill out the Free Application for Federal Student Aid.

According to Federal Student Aid data, approximately 18 million FAFSAs are submitted annually (down from a peak of 21.9 million applications in the 2011-2012 academic year).

The New FAFSA: Streamlined for Efficiency

The updated FAFSA, implemented in 2023, aims to simplify the application process and make it more accessible for students. The new FAFSA form is more user-friendly and streamlined than the previous version.

These are the main modifications:

Simplified Interface: The online application now has a more user-friendly interface. A redesign and reduction in the number of questions (only 36 questions compared to 108) are part of the FAFSA's makeover.

Tax Information Integration: The IRS Data Retrieval Tool automatically imports tax information, reducing manual entry and potential errors. Applicants will be required to use this IRS tool. Additionally, the FAFSA now no longer counts 401(k) contributions toward a family's income.

Simplified Dependency Status: The process for determining dependency status is streamlined, making it easier for students to qualify for aid. Parents on the FAFSA will be the custodial parent who provides the student with the most financial support and will no longer be the parent with whom the student lived with the most over the past

12 months. Email addresses or mobile phone numbers are required. Also, know the value of family businesses or farms if you own one.

Students can track their application status and view their official FAFSA Submission Summary through their StudentAid.gov account. Paper submissions may take 7–10 days to process, with notifications sent by email or mail.

The Department of Education said the new FAFSA should help "610,000 more students from low-income backgrounds receive Pell Grants." That is the hope. Pell Grants have experienced a significant decline in recent years.

Once the application is complete, students will receive a confirmation email including their estimated Student Aid Index and Pell Grant eligibility. Students and families will also be able to download the form and mail it to the Department of Education3.

You can find more information about the FAFSA application on the Federal Student Aid website.

Question 8

What is the correct answer to question 8 on the FAFSA: "Are the student's parents unwilling to provide their information?" The correct answer to question 8 for most students is "No." Checking "Yes" will exclude students from Pell Grants and most other federal student aid.

About Pell Grants

In Appendix A (College Financial Planning Terms), Pell Grants is defined as: "A need-based federal grant awarded to undergraduate students to help cover educational expenses." This grant has no repayment requirement, which pays for tuition, housing, and board.

The way Pell Grants are discussed at times, you would think almost everyone qualifies. This is far from the truth. It depends upon your need and other factors. For example, while 31% of students at public 4-year universities receive the grant, only 13% of students at private 4-year universities receive one. This is a considerable difference, meaning students need to adjust their expectations accordingly. Undergraduates who received federal Pell Grants received an average of $4,100 according, to the U.S. Department of Education's Institute of Education Sciences (IES).

An additional problem with this grant, and this data, is that far fewer students are receiving fewer students receive federal Pell Grants compared to just five or ten years ago. Approximately 6 million students are awarded Pell Grants today compared with a high of 9.4 million students in 2011, a little over ten years ago. Tuition costs continue to climb, while Pell Grants have rapidly declined. Why has this reduced funding happened? Call your local member of Congress, maybe they can tell you. Today, you need to clearly prove your low-income status or be very fortunate to receive a federal Pell Grant.

More Recommendations

Completing the Free Application for Federal Student Aid (FAFSA) is crucial for students seeking financial assistance for college in the United States. Here are the top ten recommendations for completing the FAFSA application:

1. Gather Necessary Documents: Gather all essential documents beforehand, including your Social Security number, federal income tax returns, W-2s, bank statements, and records of any untaxed income.

2. Create an FSA ID: Both the student and one parent (if dependent) should create a Federal Student Aid (FSA) ID at fsaid.ed.gov. This

ID is used to sign the FAFSA and access other federal aid websites electronically.

3. Start Early and Know Deadlines: Ensure you complete it as early as possible to meet federal, state, and college deadlines, as some funds are distributed on a first-come, first-served basis.

4. Use the Official FAFSA Website: Access the official FAFSA website at fafsa.ed.gov or via the myStudentAid app. Avoid third-party sites that charge fees, as the FAFSA is entirely free.

5. Provide Accurate Information: Complete the FAFSA accurately. Double-check all entered information, including personal details, financial information, and school codes. Mistakes can cause delays or result in inaccurate aid offers.

6. List Colleges Correctly: Include all colleges you're applying to on the FAFSA. This ensures they receive your financial aid information and can provide appropriate aid packages.

7. Understand Dependency Status: Be aware of your dependency status. Dependent students must provide parental information, while independent students do not require this information.

8. Utilize the IRS Data Retrieval Tool (DRT): If eligible, use the IRS DRT within the FAFSA form to automatically import your and your parents' tax information. This helps reduce errors and simplifies the process.

9. Review and Submit: Before submission, review the entire application thoroughly to ensure accuracy and completeness. Then, submit the FAFSA electronically as soon as it's ready.

10. Follow Up and Stay Informed: After submission, monitor your email and the student aid report (SAR) for any required corrections or additional information requests. Respond promptly to any inquiries.

Additionally, it's essential to research and understand the different types of financial aid available, such as grants, scholarships, work-study programs, and federal loans. This knowledge can help you make informed decisions when evaluating your aid options.

Remember, completing the FAFSA is just the beginning of the financial aid process. Stay in contact with your college's financial aid office for guidance and updates throughout your academic journey.

Tackling Common Challenges:

While filling out the FAFSA, Gen Z might face challenges:

Lack of financial information: Gathering accurate financial information from parents can be difficult for young dependents. Open communication and collaboration are key.

Understanding complex terminology: Unfamiliar financial terms can be confusing. Utilize online resources and guidance from financial aid counselors.

Meeting deadlines: With busy schedules and competing priorities, timely submission can be challenging. Set reminders and prioritize completing the FAFSA early.

Maximizing Your Aid: Strategies for Success

Gen Z can maximize their financial aid by:

Exploring all grant opportunities: Grants, unlike loans, don't require repayment. Research federal, state, and institution-specific grants based on academic achievements, financial need, and specific interests.

Considering work-study programs: These programs provide part-time employment opportunities while attending college, allowing students to earn money and gain valuable work experience.

Negotiating with colleges: After receiving financial aid offers, compare them across different institutions and initiate dialogues with financial aid offices to potentially negotiate better packages.

Exploring Alternative Financial Aid Avenues

Beyond traditional federal aid, Gen Z can explore alternative options:

Scholarships: Numerous private organizations and foundations offer scholarships based on academic merit, community involvement, or specific talents. Research and apply to relevant scholarships to supplement financial aid packages.

Private loans: Private loans can be a last resort option to bridge the gap between financial aid and the total cost of attendance. Carefully compare interest rates and repayment terms before choosing a private lender.

State and local grants: Many states and localities offer grant programs to support students pursuing higher education. Research available programs in your area and meet any specific eligibility requirements.

The FAFSA serves as a crucial gateway to financial aid, paving the path for Gen Z to pursue higher education without crippling debt. By understanding the application process, tackling challenges head-on, and exploring alternative options, they can maximize their financial aid opportunities and make informed decisions about their future.

Navigating the FAFSA may seem complex, but it's not insurmountable. By utilizing resources, seeking guidance, and proactively exploring options, *Gen Z can unlock the doors to financial aid and achieve their educational aspirations.*

Parents

Simply said, parents should always fill out the Free Application for Federal Student Aid (FAFSA) since they can never tell what kind of financial aid their child may need or require. No matter how much money your family generates, this will still be true.

The FAFSA allows students to access state grants, federal grants, and student loans, which typically have better terms than anything they would get privately.

Also, if a parent has lost their job or has experienced high medical debt, gather the supporting documents to show schools these exceptional circumstances in determining financial aid.

This is very easy to accomplish: "The student may want to use the Federal Student Aid Estimator before filling out the FAFSA® form to help them understand their options for paying for college or career school by providing them an early estimate of how much federal student aid they may be eligible for."

https://studentaid.gov/aid-estimator/

If a student's parent(s) decline to submit the FAFSA, the student ought to discuss the reasons for their refusal with the college's financial aid administrator. Financial aid administrators may occasionally be able to allay and even mollify the parents' worries and persuade them to finish the application.

When people's feelings are involved, conversations about money and families can get heated. Feelings of shame, anxiety, regret, and a host of others may surface. But here a young person's future hangs in the balance. And this educational decision does not come close in importance compared to buying a smart phone or even a vehicle. A college degree can be an asset that produces lifetime benefits.

Parents ... what about the scenario of "Johnny or Susie come lately?" What does this mean? Can you explain this to me? It means that not all students progress at the rate or conform to our expectations. This reality should be rather obvious.

Consider the case of a lackadaisical, underperforming, and disinterested "C" student in high school. Meaning they don't care about their grades or extracurricular activities. This student is not sold on the academic system or world. (With grade inflation in today's schools, a "C" student is underperforming.) As a senior, our student suddenly wakes up and smells the espresso. This student, now aware of their future beyond high school, starts to perform well and exhibits some newly found motivation. Would it be fair to deny this youngster the chance to attend college because of their low grades before senior year?

To find Late Bloomers, look them up online. Countless interesting anecdotes and illustrations await you. It has no age limit.

The publishers of this book know of students who were misdiagnosed in high school and became respected medical doctors and other professionals. They also know of those who could barely write a three-page report and became gifted, star athletes in college and professional life.

Stay Informed

To receive updates, log in to your StudentAid.gov account often to monitor your status.

Follow Federal Student Aid on social media for resources and announcements.

Twitter

Instagram

Facebook

YouTube (Informational Videos)

YouTube (Educational Webinars)

studentaid.gov

Chapter 17: Scholarships

The Basics

Gen Z students should understand that full-ride scholarships are highly competitive and relatively rare (except for need-based students). Less than one percent of students enrolling in college will get one. It's important to note that while full-ride scholarships can be difficult to obtain, many students receive partial scholarships or other forms of financial aid to help offset the cost of college.

Students who are in the top ten percent of their class have a higher probability and a great chance of obtaining a scholarship (albeit a partial scholarship). Students who think they are at the top of their class should apply.

Some departments and clubs in colleges have a scholarship budget set aside for their activities. For example, a college debate team may have ten thousand or twenty thousand dollars set aside for scholarships each year. Five or ten students may be recipients of a debate scholarship each year. We suggest calling and meeting with the professor in charge of the debate team for further information.

Time, energy, creative writing, and dedication are required for an active personal campaign to win scholarships.

As students and their families navigate the complex landscape of higher education financing, explore every available option to minimize debt and maximize financial aid. Scholarships and grants are two of the most significant sources of free money that can significantly reduce the financial burden of pursuing a higher education. This chapter will delve into the world of scholarships and grants, identifying, applying for, and securing these valuable opportunities.

What are Scholarships and Grants?

Scholarships and grants are forms of financial aid that do not need to be repaid. Scholarships are typically awarded based on academic merit, talent, or other specific criteria, while grants are often awarded based on financial need. Both scholarships and grants can be offered by a wide range of organizations, including colleges and universities, private foundations, corporations, and government agencies.

Types of Scholarships and Grants

1. Merit-Based Scholarships: Awarded based on academic achievement, talent, or other specific criteria. (read Appendix E: Merit Based Scholarships)

2. Need-Based Grants: These are awarded based on financial need, as determined by the Free Application for Federal Student Aid (FAFSA). Pell Grants is an example.

3. Merit-Based Grants: Awarded based on academic achievement, talent, or other specific criteria but do not require financial need.

4. Private Scholarships: Awarded by private organizations, foundations, and corporations.

5. Government Grants: Awarded by federal, state, and local government agencies.

6. Institutional Grants: Awarded by colleges and universities to their students.

7. External Grants: Awarded by external organizations, such as private foundations and corporations.

Scholarship Search and Application Plan for US Universities:

Early Steps (9th-10th Grade):

Explore Potential Majors and Colleges: Start broad, then narrow down your interests. Research universities offering programs that align with your goals.

Identify Scholarship Types: Merit-based (academics, achievements), need-based (financial aid), identity-based (ethnicity, background), and talent-based (arts, athletics).

Create a Scholarship Master List: Track each scholarship's deadlines, eligibility requirements, and application materials. Use platforms like Fastweb, Scholarships.com, and college websites.

Focused Preparation (11th Grade):

Boost Academics: Maintain a high GPA, take challenging courses, and score well on standardized tests (SAT/ACT). Consider AP/IB exams for potential college credit.

Develop Activities and Achievements: Participate in extracurriculars, leadership roles, community service, competitions, internships, or projects related to your major and scholarship interests.

Build Relationships: Seek recommendation letters from teachers, counselors, and advisors who can speak to your strengths and potential.

Application Process (Senior Year):

Refine Scholarship List: Prioritize based on eligibility, application requirements, and potential award amount. Aim for a mix of reach, match, and safety scholarships.

Gather Application Materials: Prepare transcripts, test scores, recommendation letters, essays, financial aid documents (FAFSA), and portfolios (if applicable) well in advance of deadlines.

Meet Deadlines: Be organized and proactive. Set calendar reminders and submit applications before deadlines to avoid disqualification.

Tips for Writing Effective Scholarship Applications

Securing scholarships often requires more than just meeting eligibility criteria; it involves crafting compelling applications that stand out to scholarship committees. Tailor your essay to each scholarship, highlighting unique experiences, achievements, and goals relevant to the specific scholarship and university. Showcase your passions and potential impact. Here are some tips for writing effective scholarship applications:

Start Early:

Begin your scholarship search and application process early. Deadlines vary, and some scholarships have deadlines, so starting early gives you ample time to find opportunities and complete applications.

Understand the Requirements:

Carefully read the eligibility criteria and application requirements for each scholarship. Ensure you meet all the criteria before applying and gather all necessary documents and information.

Tailor Your Application:

Customize each application to align with the scholarship's goals and values. Highlight experiences, achievements, and goals that match the scholarship's criteria.

Write a Strong Personal Statement:

Your personal statement is your opportunity to tell your story and explain why you deserve the scholarship. Be authentic, highlight your achievements, discuss challenges you've overcome, and outline your future goals.

Example Structure:

Introduction: Start with a compelling hook or anecdote.

Body: Discuss your background, achievements, and experiences.

Conclusion: Outline your future goals and explain how the scholarship will help you achieve them.

Showcase Your Achievements:

Highlight academic achievements, extracurricular activities, community service, leadership roles, and any relevant work experience. Provide specific examples and quantify your accomplishments when possible.

Obtain Strong Letters of Recommendation:

Choose recommenders who know you well and can speak to your strengths and potential. Give them information about the scholarship and your achievements to help them write detailed and supportive letters.

Proofread and Edit:

Review your application materials carefully. Check for grammar and spelling errors, and ensure your application is well-organized and free of typos. Consider asking a teacher, mentor, or family member to review your application before submitting it.

Follow Instructions:

Adhere to all application instructions, including word limits, formatting requirements, and submission guidelines. Failure to follow instructions can result in disqualification.

Realistic Expectations:

As noted, scholarship applications are highly competitive exercises. Some will suggest applying to many opportunities, even if they seem like "long shots." Realistically, that will bring about much frustration. Others will suggest focusing on quality over quantity. Invest time and effort into applications that align with your profile and goals—a more targeted approach.

Scholarships are arguably the most valuable form of financial aid. They offer free money that doesn't need to be repaid, making them a crucial component of your debt-free strategy.

Understand there are many factors beyond your control in the selection process. Celebrate every application submitted and scholarship received.

Additional Tips:

Utilize Scholarship Search Engines: Platforms like Fastweb, Scholarships.com, and Unigo offer extensive databases of scholarships based on your academic performance, interests, and background.

Explore College and State-Specific Scholarships: Many universities and state governments offer scholarships specifically for their students. Research and apply to these opportunities early.

Target Niche Scholarships: Don't limit yourself to general scholarships. Look for scholarships specific to your major, ethnicity, extracurricular activities, or hobbies.

Seek Employer-Sponsored Scholarships: Some employers offer scholarships to their employees' children or dependents. Inquire with your parents' workplaces for potential opportunities.

Write Compelling Essays: Many scholarships require application essays. Invest time crafting compelling and personalized essays highlighting your unique story and achievements.

Crowdfunding: Leverage your network for support. Platforms like GoFundMe and Kickstarter allow you to raise funds from your network of friends, family, and even strangers.

Other tips: Attend college fairs and scholarship workshops for guidance and networking opportunities. Connect with current students or alumni from your high school or desired universities for insights.

Manage stress and expectations: Stay positive and focused, and remember that scholarships are just one piece of the college funding puzzle.

Securing scholarships and grants requires a strategic and proactive approach. By understanding the types of scholarships and grants available, utilizing online resources, and applying a systematic approach to the application process, students can maximize their chances of securing free money to fund their higher education. Remember to start early, be persistent, and customize your applications to increase your chances of success. By doing so, students can reduce their financial burden, achieve their academic goals, and set themselves up for long-term financial success.

Please note: This is a general guide. Specific details and strategies may vary depending on your circumstances and chosen universities. Always refer to the official scholarship websites and university financial aid offices for the most up-to-date information and requirements.

On Campus: Embrace the Power of Frugal Living

While finding alternative funding is crucial, minimizing your overall expenses is equally important. Embrace frugality by adopting these strategies:

Create a budget and track your spending.

Live within your means and avoid unnecessary expenses.

Utilize student discounts and resources.

Cook at home instead of eating out frequently.

Borrow or buy used textbooks instead of purchasing new ones.

Explore free or low-cost entertainment options.

By embracing these creative funding strategies and practicing mindful spending, Gen Z can navigate the financial challenges of higher education and achieve their academic aspirations without falling into the trap of crippling student debt. Remember, the key lies in strategic planning, proactive action, and a commitment to financial responsibility.

Florida: The Programs of Strategic Emphasis (PSE)

The PSE list helps provide highly qualified talent to support Florida's most critical workforce shortages. It also serves as a valuable resource for students to select majors that offer a positive return on investment.

Some of the current programs of strategic emphasis include:

Computer & Information Sciences

Information Technology

Civil Engineering

There is a long list of majors that qualify including physics, finance and elementary education. Previously, this was known as STEM waiver. The Florida program applies to all Florida state universities for residents of Florida. This is a 50% tuition waiver applied to certain, but not all courses. This waiver can significantly reduce the cost of education for students in these high-demand fields.

Unique Scholarships

There are many interesting, unique, and even weird scholarships available for students. Have you ever heard of ..... ?

The Evans Caddie Scholarship. This scholarship covers full tuition and housing costs for four years for students who have successfully and regularly been golf caddies for at least the past two years.

In 2024, two students from Colorado won Division I scholarships for cornhole, the popular backyard game. Yes, you read this correctly, cornhole. These students are taking their bad tossing skills to Winthrop University in South Carolina. So popular is cornhole that ESPN continues to broadcast American Cornhole League (ACL) events as a growing and thriving sport. The league tagline is: "Anyone can play, anyone can win."

Below are some more interesting scholarships:

Niche-Specific Scholarships

Tall Clubs International Foundation Scholarship: For exceptionally tall students.

American Association of Candy Technologists Scholarship: For students interested in food science.

The Vegetarian Resource Group College Scholarship: For students who have promoted vegetarianism.

Scholars Helping Collars Scholarship: This scholarship is for students passionate about animal welfare.

Creative and Unusual Scholarships

Create-A-Greeting-Card Scholarship Contest: Rewards creativity and design skills.

Minecraft Scholarship: Recognizes Minecraft expertise and academic achievement.

No Essay Scholarship: Offers financial aid without requiring an essay.

Zombie Apocalypse Scholarship: Rewards students who have a plan to survive a zombie apocalypse.

Chapter 18: Free Tuition

According to our most recent research, the colleges listed below offer free college tuition.

Free tuition??? Yes! Yes, you read that right. Some American universities provide tuition-free programs. (However, please note that tuition policies can change, and new programs may have been introduced.)

As you well know, the total cost of attending college includes more than just tuition. Free tuition is available with the colleges noted in this chapter. In most cases, it does not cover living expenses, meals, or any supplemental costs for students.

The following institutions make claims of being tuition-free, although there are conditions and restrictions associated with these possible offers of admission.

Additionally, these noted institutions are not suitable for everyone. Some have very low acceptance rates, are located in rural areas, are faith-based, involve job programs, or have income requirements for households.

You must reside in specific rural counties to attend one of these colleges (Alice Lloyd). Some schools demand that students qualify for the Federal Pell Grant (requiring a FAFSA). A particular institution asks you to "Become a craftsman during a minimum 7,000 hours of on-the-job training in one of 19 shipbuilding disciplines." (The Apprentice School). Wow! What do you think?

"Exceptionally gifted young musicians" are accepted by schools such as the Curtis Institute of Music. Military schools, however, have their own stringent criteria. It is wise to know a member of congress for these schools. Also, it is good to know that midshipmen at the U.S. Naval Academy also get a monthly stipend of at least $1200 for extra personal expenses.

We anticipate that the greater majority of students will skim this list, after looking at it once, and decide "no thanks, not for me" for a variety of reasons. Then again, you never know.

Alice Lloyd College

Pippa Passes, KY

https://www.alc.edu/

Alice Lloyd College offers free tuition to students from its 108-county service area in Central Appalachia. The college was founded to serve students from this region, and its donors have generously provided funding to cover the cost of tuition for all qualified students. The college's mission places a strong emphasis on community service.

In addition to free tuition, Alice Lloyd College also offers a number of other financial aid opportunities, including scholarships, grants, and work-study. Students are also encouraged to complete the Free Application for Federal Student Aid (FAFSA) to see if they qualify for any federal aid.

Antioch College

Yellow Springs, OH

https://antiochcollege.edu/

Antioch College is a private liberal arts college in Yellow Springs, Ohio. It was founded in 1852 by Horace Mann and was the first coeducational college in the United States. The college's curriculum is designed to be practical and relevant to the needs of students.

Antioch College offers a variety of undergraduate programs, including majors in the arts, sciences, humanities, and social sciences. The college also offers a number of graduate programs, including master's degrees in education, business administration, and environmental studies.

In addition to its academic programs, Antioch College is also known for its commitment to social justice and its focus on experiential learning. The college has a long history of activism, and its students have been involved in a number of social justice movements, including the civil rights movement and the anti-war movement.

The Apprentice School

Newport News, VA

https://www.as.edu/

The Apprentice School is a private, non-profit trade school in Newport News, Virginia, United States. Founded in 1919, it is the #1 Trade School in the U.S. They offer programs in shipbuilding, and students can earn while they learn.

The Apprentice School offers a unique educational experience that combines classroom learning with hands-on experience in the field. Students earn a paycheck while they learn, and they graduate with the skills and experience they need to succeed in the shipbuilding industry.

Barclay College

Haviland, KS

https://www.barclaycollege.edu/

Barclay College is a Christian college located in Haviland, Kansas. The college offers a variety of bachelor's degrees, associate's degrees, and certificates. Barclay College is known for its small class sizes and welcoming community.

Barclay College does offer free tuition, but only for students who live on campus. This is called the Full Tuition Scholarship and it covers the full cost of tuition for all students who live in the dorms. Students are still responsible for room and board, as well as general and technology fees.

Berea College

Berea, KY

https://www.berea.edu/

Berea College is a private liberal arts college located in Berea, Kentucky. The college was founded in 1855 and is the first integrated, co-educational college in the South. Berea College has not charged students tuition since 1892. It primarily focuses on serving students from low-income backgrounds.

Instead of paying tuition, students are required to work on campus to help offset the cost of their education. This work program is a key part of the Berea College experience and helps students develop valuable skills and experience.

Berea College offers a variety of undergraduate programs, including majors in the arts, sciences, humanities, and social sciences. The college also offers a number of graduate programs, including master's degrees in education and social work.

College of the Ozarks

Point Lookout, MO

https://www.cofo.edu/

College of the Ozarks is a private, Christian, liberal arts college located in Point Lookout, Missouri. The college was founded in 1906 and is dedicated to providing a Christian education for students who are worthy but lack the means.

The college offers a variety of undergraduate programs, including majors in the arts, sciences, humanities, and social sciences. The college also offers a number of graduate programs, including master's degrees in education and business administration.

Students at College of the Ozarks are required to work on campus in exchange for their education. This work program helps to offset the cost of tuition and provides students with valuable work experience.

The college is known for its beautiful campus, which is located in the Ozark Mountains. The campus is home to a number of historic buildings, as well as a variety of recreational facilities.

Curtis Institute of Music

Philadelphia, PA

https://www.curtis.edu/

The Curtis Institute of Music, located in Philadelphia, Pennsylvania, is a highly selective and prestigious conservatory known for its exceptional music education and its unique commitment to providing free tuition to all students. As one of the most prestigious music schools in the country. It is known for its rigorous training programs for musicians.

Founded in 1924, Curtis has a long history of nurturing the talents of some of the world's most renowned musicians. Alumni include Leonard Bernstein, Lang Lang, Samuel Barber, and Gian Carlo Menotti, just to name a few.

Here are some key points about Curtis Institute of Music:

Admissions: Admission to Curtis is highly competitive, with only a few dozen students accepted each year. The application process involves a pre-screening audition, followed by live auditions in Philadelphia.

Free Tuition: All students admitted to Curtis receive a full-tuition scholarship, regardless of their financial need. This allows students to focus on their studies without the burden of tuition debt.

Academic Programs: Curtis offers a comprehensive curriculum that includes instrumental and vocal performance, composition, conducting, and music theory. Students also have the opportunity to participate in a variety of ensembles and chamber groups.

Faculty: The faculty at Curtis consists of distinguished musicians and educators who are dedicated to providing their students with the highest quality instruction and mentorship.

Performance Opportunities: Students at Curtis have the opportunity to perform in master classes, recitals, and concerts throughout the year. They also have the opportunity to perform with the Curtis Symphony Orchestra and the Curtis Opera Theatre.

Facilities: Curtis boasts state-of-the-art facilities, including a concert hall, a recital hall, a library, and practice rooms.

Overall, Curtis Institute of Music offers students a unique opportunity to receive a world-class music education at no cost. The school's commitment to free tuition and its focus on individual attention make it a truly exceptional place to study music.

Deep Springs College

Dyer, NV

https://www.deepsprings.edu/

Deep Springs College, nestled in the remote Deep Springs Valley of Nevada, is a unique and transformative educational experience unlike any other. This tuition-free college combines a rigorous academic program with a hands-on commitment to environmental stewardship and self-governance.

Here are some key points about Deep Springs College:

Academics: The college offers a liberal arts curriculum with a focus on interdisciplinary studies. Students take courses in a variety of subjects, including literature, history, science, philosophy, and the arts. The college also offers a unique program in environmental studies, which includes hands-on experience in the college's 20,000-acre working ranch.

Labor Program: All students at Deep Springs are required to participate in the college's labor program, working 20 hours per week on the college ranch and farm. This program is a fundamental part of the Deep Springs experience, teaching students valuable skills in agriculture, animal husbandry, and self-sufficiency.

Self-Governance: Students at Deep Springs are responsible for governing themselves through a consensus-based decision-making process. This unique system teaches students valuable skills in leadership, communication, and collaboration.

Community: Deep Springs is a close-knit community where students live, work, and learn together. This fosters a strong sense of belonging and camaraderie among students.

Location: The college's remote location in the Nevada desert provides a unique and challenging environment for students to learn and grow. The natural beauty of the surrounding area offers opportunities for outdoor activities and exploration.

Free Tuition: Deep Springs offers free tuition to all students, making it an accessible option for students from all backgrounds.

Haskell Indian Nations University

Lawrence, KS

https://www.haskell.edu/

Haskell Indian Nations University (HINU), located in Lawrence, Kansas, is a unique and historic institution dedicated to providing a quality education for Native American students. Founded in 1884, Haskell is the only federally funded tribal university in the United States, offering free tuition to all enrolled members of federally recognized tribes.

Here are some key points about Haskell Indian Nations University:

Mission: Haskell's mission is to "provide a culturally-enriching and intellectually stimulating environment where Tribal Nations' values and perspectives are integrated into a holistic learning experience." This mission is reflected in the university's curriculum, which emphasizes

Indigenous cultures, languages, and traditions alongside traditional academic disciplines.

Academics: Haskell offers a diverse range of undergraduate programs, including majors in the arts, sciences, humanities, business, and education. The university also offers a number of master's degrees and graduate certificates.

Cultural Programs: Haskell offers a rich array of cultural programs and activities that celebrate Indigenous cultures and traditions. This includes pow wows, language classes, traditional arts workshops, and guest speakers.

Student Life: Haskell fosters a strong sense of community among its students. The university offers a variety of clubs and organizations, social events, and recreational activities.

Location: Lawrence, Kansas, offers a vibrant college town atmosphere with a variety of cultural attractions, shopping, and dining options.

Free Tuition: One of the most distinctive features of Haskell is its commitment to providing free tuition to all enrolled members of federally recognized tribes. This makes Haskell an accessible option for Native American students who are seeking a quality education.

United States Air Force Academy

USAF Academy, CO

https://www.usafa.edu/

The United States Air Force Academy: A World-Class Education with Free Tuition

The United States Air Force Academy (USAFA), located in Colorado Springs, Colorado, is a renowned institution that offers a free tuition, world-class education to students who are committed to serving as officers in the United States Air Force. The Academy's rigorous academic program, combined with its emphasis on leadership, character development, and physical fitness, prepares its graduates for successful careers in the military and beyond.

Here are some key points about the United States Air Force Academy:

Academics: The USAFA offers a rigorous academic program that includes courses in the arts, sciences, humanities, and engineering. Students also complete a comprehensive core curriculum that focuses on leadership, ethics, and military history. The Academy boasts a low student-to-faculty ratio, allowing for personalized attention and mentorship.

Military Training: In addition to their academic studies, cadets at the USAFA participate in a comprehensive military training program. This program includes physical fitness training, military drills, and leadership development exercises. Cadets also have the opportunity to participate in a variety of extracurricular activities, including flying clubs, sports teams, and community service projects.

Character Development: The USAFA places a strong emphasis on character development. Cadets are expected to adhere to the Academy's Honor Code, which emphasizes honesty, integrity, and respect. The Academy also provides a variety of resources and programs to help cadets develop their leadership skills, communication skills, and sense of responsibility.

Physical Fitness: Cadets at the USAFA are required to maintain a high level of physical fitness. They participate in regular physical training sessions and compete in a variety of intramural and varsity sports. The

Academy's physical fitness program helps cadets develop the strength, endurance, and agility they need to succeed in the military.

Free Tuition: One of the most attractive features of the USAFA is its free tuition. In exchange for their commitment to serve in the Air Force, cadets receive a full scholarship that covers the cost of their education. This makes the Academy a financially accessible option for students who are interested in a military career.

Overall, the United States Air Force Academy offers a unique and challenging educational experience that prepares students for successful careers in the military and beyond. The Academy's commitment to academics, military training, character development, and physical fitness produces well-rounded graduates who are ready to serve their country with honor and distinction.

United States Coast Guard Academy

New London, CT

https://uscga.edu/

United States Coast Guard Academy: A Rewarding Education with Free Tuition

The United States Coast Guard Academy (USCGA), located in New London, Connecticut, is a unique and prestigious institution that offers a free tuition, world-class education to students who are committed to serving as officers in the United States Coast Guard. The Academy provides a challenging academic program, extensive leadership training, and a strong emphasis on character development, preparing graduates for diverse and rewarding careers in the Coast Guard and beyond.

Here are some key points about the United States Coast Guard Academy:

Academics: The USCGA offers a rigorous academic program leading to a Bachelor of Science degree in one of nine major fields of study, including engineering, marine science, government, and management. The curriculum emphasizes problem-solving, critical thinking, and communication skills, while also incorporating hands-on learning experiences and opportunities for independent research.

Leadership Training: Integral to the USCGA experience is its comprehensive leadership training. Cadets develop leadership skills through classroom instruction, practical exercises, and participation in a variety of extracurricular activities, including athletics, clubs, and community service projects. The Academy fosters a culture of teamwork and collaboration, preparing graduates to lead effectively in complex and challenging situations.

Character Development: The USCGA upholds a strong commitment to character development. Cadets are expected to adhere to the Academy's Honor Concept, which emphasizes honesty, integrity, and respect. The Academy provides a supportive environment and resources to help cadets develop strong ethical values, a sense of responsibility, and a commitment to serving others.

Physical Fitness: Cadets at the USCGA maintain a high level of physical fitness through a demanding physical training program. This program includes regular exercise sessions, participation in intramural and varsity sports, and rigorous seamanship training. The emphasis on physical fitness ensures graduates are prepared for the physically demanding aspects of Coast Guard service.

Free Tuition: A major benefit of attending the USCGA is its free tuition. In exchange for their commitment to serve in the Coast Guard after graduation, cadets receive a full scholarship that covers the cost of their education. This makes the Academy a financially accessible option for students who are interested in a meaningful career serving their country.

Overall, the United States Coast Guard Academy offers a unique opportunity for students to receive a high-quality education, develop strong leadership skills, and serve their country in a rewarding career. The Academy's dedication to academics, leadership training, character development, and physical fitness prepares graduates to become well-rounded individuals who can make a positive impact on the world.

United States Merchant Marine Academy

Kings Point, NY

https://www.usmma.edu/

The United States Merchant Marine Academy (USMMA), located in Kings Point, New York, is a federal service academy that offers a free tuition, world-class education to students who are committed to serving as officers in the United States Merchant Marine. The Academy provides a rigorous academic program, extensive sea experience, and a strong emphasis on leadership training, preparing graduates for challenging and rewarding careers at sea and ashore.

Here are some key points about the United States Merchant Marine Academy:

Academics: The USMMA offers a rigorous academic program leading to a Bachelor of Science degree in one of six major fields of study, including marine engineering, marine transportation, and logistics and intermodal transportation. The curriculum emphasizes technical knowledge, professional skills, and critical thinking, preparing graduates for diverse roles within the maritime industry.

Sea Experience: A unique aspect of the USMMA experience is its extensive sea experience. Midshipmen (students) embark on a year-long training cruise aboard commercial vessels, gaining practical experience in various aspects of shipboard operations. This real-world exposure prepares graduates for the demands of working at sea and fosters a strong understanding of maritime operations.

Leadership Training: The USMMA emphasizes leadership development through a variety of programs and activities. Midshipmen receive instruction in leadership principles, participate in practical exercises, and hold leadership positions within the regimental structure. This training equips graduates with the skills and confidence to lead effectively in complex maritime environments.

Character Development: The USMMA fosters a culture of honesty, integrity, and responsibility. Midshipmen are expected to adhere to the Academy's Honor Code and uphold high ethical standards. The Academy provides opportunities for personal reflection, ethical decision-making, and service to others, fostering well-rounded individuals who are prepared to serve with honor.

Physical Fitness: Midshipmen at the USMMA maintain a high level of physical fitness through a demanding physical training program. This program includes regular exercise sessions, participation in intramural sports, and shipboard physical training. The emphasis on physical fitness ensures graduates are prepared for the physically demanding aspects of maritime service.

Free Tuition: A major advantage of attending the USMMA is its free tuition. In exchange for their commitment to serve in the United States Merchant Marine after graduation, midshipmen receive a full scholarship that covers the cost of their education. This makes the Academy a financially accessible option for students who are interested in a rewarding career at sea.

Overall, the United States Merchant Marine Academy offers a unique and valuable educational experience for students who are passionate about the maritime industry. The Academy's commitment to academics, sea experience, leadership training, character development, and physical fitness prepares graduates to become skilled professionals and leaders who contribute to the global maritime industry.

United States Military Academy

West Point, NY

https://www.westpoint.edu/

United States Military Academy: Leading the Way with Free Education

The United States Military Academy (USMA), more commonly known as West Point, is a prestigious four-year federal service academy located in West Point, New York. It offers a free tuition education to students who are committed to serving as commissioned officers in the United States Army. West Point is renowned for its rigorous academic program, emphasis on leadership development, and tradition of producing well-rounded leaders for the Army.

Here are some key points about the United States Military Academy:

Academics: The USMA offers a rigorous academic program leading to a Bachelor of Science degree in one of 34 major fields of study, including engineering, mathematics, and social sciences. The curriculum emphasizes critical thinking, problem-solving, and communication skills, preparing graduates for diverse challenges in military and civilian careers.

Leadership Development: West Point is known for its unwavering commitment to leadership development. Cadets receive extensive training in leadership principles, ethics, and decision-making through classroom instruction, practical exercises, and participation in a variety of extracurricular activities. This training instills in graduates the skills and confidence to lead effectively in complex and demanding situations.

Military Training: Cadets at West Point undergo comprehensive military training, including physical fitness conditioning, combat skills instruction, and field exercises. This training prepares graduates for the physical and mental demands of military service and equips them with the necessary skills to lead their soldiers in combat and other demanding situations.

Character Development: West Point cultivates a community based on honor, integrity, and ethical conduct. Cadets are expected to adhere to the Academy's Honor Code, which emphasizes honesty, fairness, and responsibility. This fosters a strong moral compass in graduates, ensuring they serve with distinction and uphold the highest ethical standards.

Physical Fitness: Maintaining a high level of physical fitness is essential for cadets at West Point. They participate in a demanding physical training program that includes regular exercise sessions, competitive sports, and rigorous obstacle courses. This emphasis on physical fitness ensures graduates are prepared for the physical demands of military service and possess the endurance necessary for sustained operations.

Free Tuition: One of the most attractive features of attending West Point is its free tuition. In exchange for their commitment to serve as officers in the Army, cadets receive a full scholarship that covers the cost of their education. This makes the Academy a financially accessible option for students who are passionate about leadership and service.

Overall, the United States Military Academy offers a unique and transformative educational experience that prepares students for successful careers as leaders in the Army and beyond. The Academy's commitment to academics, leadership development, military training, character development, and physical fitness produces well-rounded graduates who are ready to lead with honor and distinction.

United States Naval Academy

Annapolis, MD

https://www.usna.edu/

United States Naval Academy: Leading the Way in Maritime Leadership with Free Tuition

The United States Naval Academy (USNA), located in Annapolis, Maryland, is a prestigious service academy that offers a free tuition education to students who commit to serving as officers in the United States Navy or Marine Corps. Renowned for its rigorous academics, emphasis on leadership development, and rich naval traditions, the USNA prepares its graduates to become exceptional leaders and maritime professionals.

Here are some key points about the United States Naval Academy:

Academics: The USNA offers a rigorous academic program leading to a Bachelor of Science degree in one of 25 major fields of study, including engineering, mathematics, and oceanography. The curriculum emphasizes problem-solving, critical thinking, and communication skills, while also incorporating hands-on learning experiences and opportunities for research.

Leadership Development: The USNA is dedicated to developing strong and ethical leaders. Midshipmen (students) receive extensive training in leadership principles, decision-making, and ethics through classroom instruction, practical exercises, and participation in a variety of extracurricular activities. This fosters in graduates the skills and confidence to lead effectively in complex maritime environments.

Military Training: Midshipmen undergo comprehensive military training at the USNA. This includes physical fitness conditioning, naval science courses, and practical training aboard ships. The training prepares graduates for the physical and mental demands of military service and equips them with the necessary skills to lead sailors and Marines in combat and other demanding situations.

Professional Development: The USNA focuses on professional development for future naval officers. Midshipmen participate in seamanship training, summer cruises aboard naval vessels, and internships with various Navy and Marine Corps units. This provides them with valuable hands-on experience and prepares them for the responsibilities of a commissioned officer.

Character Development: The USNA fosters a culture of honor, integrity, and responsibility. Midshipmen are expected to adhere to the Academy's Honor Code, which emphasizes honesty, fairness, and ethical conduct. This instills in graduates a strong moral compass and ensures they serve with distinction and uphold the highest ethical standards.

Physical Fitness: Maintaining a high level of physical fitness is crucial for midshipmen at the USNA. They participate in a demanding physical training program that includes regular exercise sessions, competitive sports, and rigorous obstacle courses. This ensures graduates are prepared for the physical demands of military service and possess the endurance necessary for sustained operations at sea.

Free Tuition: One of the most significant benefits of attending the USNA is its free tuition. In exchange for their commitment to serve as officers in the Navy or Marine Corps, midshipmen receive a full scholarship that covers the cost of their education. This makes the Academy a financially accessible option for students who are passionate about maritime service and leadership.

Overall, the United States Naval Academy offers a unique and transformative educational experience that prepares students for successful careers as leaders in the Navy or Marine Corps. The Academy's commitment to academics, leadership development, military training, professional development, character development, and physical fitness produces well-rounded graduates who are ready to lead with honor and distinction in the maritime domain.

Warren Wilson College

Asheville, NC

https://www.warren-wilson.edu/

Warren Wilson College: A Unique Educational Experience with Free Tuition for NC Residents

Warren Wilson College is a private, liberal arts college located in Asheville, North Carolina. Founded in 1894, the college offers a unique educational experience that combines rigorous academics with a strong commitment to environmental stewardship and community engagement. Most notably, Warren Wilson offers free tuition to all North Carolina residents who qualify for federal or state need-based grants.

Here are some key points about Warren Wilson College:

Academics: The college offers a diverse range of undergraduate programs in the arts, sciences, humanities, and social sciences. Students also have the opportunity to design their own interdisciplinary majors. The curriculum emphasizes experiential learning and hands-on projects, with many classes incorporating service learning and work-study opportunities.

Work Program: All students at Warren Wilson are required to participate in the college's work program, contributing 10 hours per week to on-campus jobs that support the college's operations and sustainability initiatives. This program instills valuable skills in teamwork, responsibility, and environmental stewardship.

Environmental Stewardship: Warren Wilson is committed to sustainability and environmental protection. The college boasts a 1,100-acre organic farm, operates on renewable energy, and encourages responsible resource management throughout the campus.

Community Engagement: Warren Wilson fosters a strong sense of community among its students, faculty, and staff. The college encourages active engagement in campus life through a variety of clubs, organizations, and social events.

Free Tuition for NC Residents: One of the most distinctive features of Warren Wilson is its commitment to providing free tuition to all

North Carolina residents who qualify for federal or state need-based grants. This makes the college an accessible option for students from all backgrounds who are seeking a high-quality education while minimizing their financial burden.

Overall, Warren Wilson College offers a unique and transformative educational experience that emphasizes academic excellence, environmental stewardship, community engagement, and personal growth. The college's commitment to free tuition for North Carolina residents makes it a financially accessible option for students who are passionate about learning and making a positive impact on the world.

Webb Institute

Glen Cove, NY

https://www.webb.edu/

Webb Institute: Building a Future in Naval Architecture and Marine Engineering with Free Tuition

Webb Institute, located in Glen Cove, New York, is a unique and prestigious private college specializing in naval architecture and marine engineering. Established in 1889, Webb is renowned for its rigorous academic program, its commitment to hands-on learning, and its distinctive feature of offering free tuition to all enrolled students.

Here are some key points about Webb Institute:

Specialized Focus: Webb Institute offers a single Bachelor of Science degree program in naval architecture and marine engineering, providing students with a comprehensive and in-depth understanding of the design, construction, and operation of ships and other marine structures. This specialized focus allows graduates to enter the workforce with a highly sought-after skillset with excellent career prospects in the maritime industry.

Rigorous Academics: The academic program at Webb is highly rigorous and challenging, featuring a demanding curriculum that combines theoretical knowledge with practical application. Students gain valuable skills in engineering design, computational modeling, hydrodynamics, and ship construction through a combination of classroom instruction, laboratory work, and hands-on projects.

Hands-on Learning: Webb Institute emphasizes hands-on learning through its unique Model Shop program. Students work on real-world projects, designing, building, and testing small-scale models of ships and marine structures. This hands-on experience provides invaluable practical knowledge and enhances students' understanding of theoretical concepts.

Faculty Expertise: Webb boasts a distinguished faculty of experienced naval architects and marine engineers who are committed to providing students with a personalized and supportive learning environment. The faculty's expertise ensures that students receive the highest quality education and are well-prepared for successful careers.

Free Tuition: A defining feature of Webb Institute is its commitment to providing free tuition to all enrolled students. This makes a Webb education accessible to students from diverse backgrounds, regardless of their financial circumstances.

Strong Alumni Network: Webb Institute alumni form a strong and supportive network that provides valuable career guidance and mentorship to current students. The alumni network also offers access to internships, job opportunities, and lifelong connections within the maritime industry.

Overall, Webb Institute offers a unique and transformative educational experience for students passionate about pursuing careers in naval architecture and marine engineering. The college's rigorous academics, hands-on learning opportunities, renowned faculty, and commitment to free tuition make it an exceptional choice for students who are driven to excel in this specialized field.

Chapter 19: Credit Cards

Target Demographic: YOU

Yes, credit card companies love college students. You, a Gen Z student, are a prime marketing prospect. Why? They begin a financial relationship with you, at an early age, which can last years. Also, if you run up your credit card, your parents could bail you out. Ultimately, card companies are going to make money off of you over time. Count on that.

The first thing to come to mind when we say "credit card" has got to be the word: DEBT. Debt is a bad four-letter word. The borrower is "Slave to the Lender." There is a cost associated with debt, called interest. That is also a bad thing. Interest gets added onto debt and also has to be paid back.

Since our ideal college student (YOU), under perfect and goal oriented circumstances, will have ZERO DEBT when they graduate college, credit cards need to be very carefully managed. Wisely using credit cards is the key. The risk of overspending and spiraling debt is only too real. Develop the right mindset, be disciplined, and put your plan into action.

We are not suggesting you not get a credit card. One or two credit cards with a total credit limit of maybe $1000-2000 dollars may be manageable and may work (assuming you have the right financial mindset). It is always nice to have the financial flexibility to purchase items such as various tech devices and plane tickets when needed. But, the question remains (since you have bought into the zero debt philosophy) where is the income or revenue or cash going to come from to PAY OFF the credit card when the bill comes in the mail next month.

Well? What is your answer? If you are working and have a job and/or have one or more side gigs in place, well then, that is the correct answer because income and cash flow ultimately solves many problems. You are certainly not going to pay off your credit cards with your student loans!

Credit Card at 18

Yes, once you turn 18, you can open a credit card account as the primary cardholder. There maybe income stipulations and other requirements depending upon the type of card you are applying for. Approval rates vary depending upon individual circumstances.

There are three main types of credit cards for you:

1. secured credit cards: this card can be opened with a refundable security deposit (which varies with each card; say, $200 or $300 upfront), which then becomes your credit limit. You may be able to earn reward and may be offered a path to upgrading to a regular, unsecured credit card. These cards are the easiest to get.

2. student credit cards: you must be a U.S. citizen and college student to apply for these cards. Typically, these cards offer the good rates and (possibly) some rewards. Nonetheless, the Consumer Financial Protection Bureau (CFPB) reports that some of these cards come with higher fees than typical market products. Do your research.

3. regular credits cards: these are unsecured credit cards for people with limited or no credit history. Income verification and other requirements typically take place. It is not easy to qualify without a job and a credit history.

Once you have your credit card, you may be able to start earning rewards (such as cash back and air miles) and also build your credit history (with good, on time payments).

Credit Card at 21

The Credit Card Accountability, Responsibility, and Disclosure (CARD) Act of 2009 has had a significant impact on college students and campuses, particularly in the way credit card companies can market and issue credit cards to students.

The CARD Act prohibits credit card issuers from extending credit to individuals under the age of 21 unless they have a co-signer or can demonstrate an independent ability to repay the debt (i.e. income). This provision aims to protect young individuals from accumulating credit card debt without the means to pay it back.

By restricting access to credit for those under 21, the CARD Act reduces the likelihood of college students accumulating high levels of credit card debt early in their adult lives. This protection is essential in preventing financial hardships for young individuals who may not have a stable income yet.

The educational initiatives required by the CARD Act contribute to increased awareness among college students about the importance of financial responsibility and managing credit wisely.

Nevertheless, once you turn 21, on campus, off-campus, or post graduation, you are totally free to apply for and qualify for credit cards.

When Gen Zers turn 21 they are deluged with offers from seemingly the entire financial marketing world (and others). Especially credit card companies. You will be regularly pounded with regular mail, email, text messages and many digital offers of all types. Happy birthday from databases throughout the country!

Many offers are entitizing and many students take advantage of them.

Other Options

You can always be added as an authorized user on someone else's credit card (many banks have no minimum age requirement). While you'll get a card with your name, the primary cardholder (usually a parent) is legally responsible for the debt.

Should you get a co-signer (usually a parent or trusted adult) for a card? Having a co-signer can increase the likelihood of approval for a credit card, especially for students who may not have a well-established credit history or income. Most financial advisors and personal finance writers will advise against doing this. Primarily because if there are problems with the card it would impact their credit score, not the students. Additionally, there are usually better credit-building card options.

FAQ

How do I avoid credit card debt as a student?

Duh. Just simply pay off 100% of your credit card balance each month. No brainer. Or, just don't apply for a card so you won't have one!

Business Considerations

If you have a side gig, side hustle or are forming your own startup, it is a good idea to have one or two credit cards to assist you with basic business transactions and for working capital purposes. The main idea, and goal, of your side hustle is that your income is greater than your costs. Otherwise, your side hustle is just a hobby.

Chapter 20: Level Up

Hey Gen-Z! Planning your future can be overwhelming, especially regarding the "college or not college" question.

Embarking on the journey of deciding whether or not to attend college is a pivotal moment in a Gen Z individual's life. It's not just a decision about education; it's a commitment to shaping your future in a way that resonates with your unique identity. Your generation tends to be hackers. It's time to adopt a distinctly yours mindset, focusing on what works best for you rather than conforming to traditional norms.

So don't be pressured by outdated advice, let's level up your approach and find the best path for YOU.

Embrace Your Individuality

Gen Z'ers are known for their innovative and unconventional approaches to life, decisions, and opportunities. The key to navigating the college decision lies in developing a mindset that is authentically yours. Instead of following the footsteps of previous generations, harness the power of your creativity and independence to forge a path that aligns with your goals and aspirations.

Forget "Brand You," Focus on Your Story

Dump the corporate jargon. It's about building your own unique story - a journey of discovery, not a marketing campaign. Figure out what YOU want and what YOU are good at. Turn your talents into tools that empower you, not a pre-packaged persona.

The concept of "Brand You" may sound a bit boomer or corporate or outdated. If it doesn't resonate with you, that's okay. They mean by BRAND YOU is to establish yourself as a professional, reliable, productive individual. Discovering your own mission and turning your talents into a winning formula.

Level Up Your Life

Leveling up is not just a Gen Z phrase; it's a call to become the highest version of yourself. This involves enhancing various aspects of your life, from learning and workouts to activism and career pursuits. It's about shedding habits and routines that hinder your progress and embracing positive changes that propel you forward. Remember, it's not about creating a new persona; it's about uncovering a more authentic, high-vibe version of yourself.

Adopting a Growth Mindset

Delve into adopting a 'growth mindset', as explored by professors and researchers at Stanford University. This mindset emphasizes the belief that abilities and intelligence can be developed through dedication and hard work. It's a powerful tool to overcome challenges and enhance your capabilities, setting the stage for continuous improvement. Stanford's got it right: a growth mindset is your superpower. Believe that you can learn, adapt, and overcome challenges.

Keep Your Plans Private, Be Disciplined, and Take Action

Forget the motivational speeches, let's get real. Planning is cool, but action is key. Put your ideas into practice, step outside your comfort zone, and don't wait for validation. Remember, progress over perfection.

While sharing your plans with others is tempting, consider keeping them to yourself initially. Focus on disciplined action and tangible progress rather than seeking immediate validation. Understand that the journey to success is personal, and the fruits of your labor will manifest in due time.

"Follow your heart and intuition"

On June 12, 2005, Steve Jobs delivered a commencement address to the Stanford University class of 2005 on a bright sunny day in Palo Alto, California.

Although this speech was given by a Baby Boomer (Jobs was born in 1955), to a class of Millennials many years ago, some of his thoughts and words might also resonate with Gen Z. He concluded his talk by saying:

> Your time is limited, so don't waste it living someone else's life. Don't be trapped by dogma, which is living with the results of other people's thinking. Don't let the noise of others' opinions drown out your own inner voice, and most important, have the courage to follow your heart and intuition. They somehow already know what you truly want to become.

In 2005, for Apple Inc., it was the days of the iPod and the Mac Mini.

Crafting Your College Decision

Whether you choose to attend college or explore alternative paths, make the decision your own. Align it with your values, aspirations, and vision for the future. Remember, there is no one-size-fits-all approach; the most critical aspect is that your chosen path resonates with your authentic self.

In conclusion, Gen Z, it's time to embrace the power of your individuality, creativity, and independence. Craft a path that reflects your unique identity and propels you toward a future that aligns with your aspirations. The journey may be challenging, but the rewards of authenticity and self-discovery far outweigh the temporary discomfort of stepping into the unknown. Level up, embrace your growth, and forge your path distinctly and unapologetically.

There's no one-size-fits-all answer. College can be amazing, but it's just one option, not the only one. Choose the path that aligns with your goals and values, whether it's academics, trade schools, apprenticeships, or something entirely different. Make your decision your own, and own it with confidence.

Remember: This is your journey, your story, your future. Level up, step up, and chase your dreams, Gen Z style!

Chapter 21: Embracing Choices for Gen Alpha

As Gen Z ages, a new generation stands on the horizon: Generation Alpha. Born entirely in the 21st century and woven into the digital fabric of life, Gen Alpha has grown up in a world where technology is as ordinary as the air they breathe. They're part of a generation known for tech fluency, creativity, and diversity—with unique characteristics and potential. But as they face the future, they also face choices that may redefine traditional paths, especially in higher education.

The College Choice or No-College Route

The virtual, online, and meta worlds will continue to change rapidly. Which means that Gen Alpha's journey will be different than previous generations. With access to a wealth of information and resources online, it's feasible for them to become experts in their chosen fields without setting foot on a college campus.

Gen Alpha's choice between college and no college could be shaped by many factors: the availability of online learning, apprenticeships, and hands-on industry training that offer specialized skill-building. With every option laid out, from boot camps to certificate programs to virtual internships, college may feel less like a requirement and more like one of several potential paths.

The Pressure to Adapt and the Drive for Personalization

Personalization in education has also reached new heights, and Gen Alpha, already comfortable with customized digital experiences, expects nothing less from their education. They may value pathways that allow them to focus intensely on a niche of interest rather than broad generalist degrees. For those who choose college, the experience might look very different from what we know today: smaller, tailored programs, hybrid in-person and digital coursework, and ongoing learning modules rather than a one-time degree. For those who opt out, the road to success could be paved with specialized courses, expert-led workshops, and real-world experience gathered through freelance projects and hands-on involvement.

A World Full of Choices, But No Clear Map

Unlike previous generations, who generally followed structured paths, Gen Alpha is stepping into a world where "success" isn't a one-size-fits-all concept. There's a chance they may find it liberating—able to carve out careers that align perfectly with their talents and interests. Yet, it's also a daunting prospect: without a single "right" choice, they may feel the weight of finding their way in a constantly evolving world.

And while skipping college may tempt Gen Alpha, they'll need to weigh the potential sacrifices. College, after all, offers more than an education; it provides a network, a space for self-discovery, and a stepping stone into professional circles. Choosing a different route could mean finding new ways to make connections and establish credibility. It's a decision that will be highly personal, and there's no doubt they'll consider it carefully.

The Role of Technology in Making Choices

As digital natives, Gen Alpha is perfectly positioned to leverage technology for making informed decisions. They may use AI-driven insights, predictive tools, and extensive data to guide them toward paths that suit their interests and aptitudes. They have an advantage over previous generations, with more resources to understand and shape their futures. However, technology, while empowering, doesn't make the choices easier. It adds to the complexity, making them acutely aware of every available option and the challenges of each path.

Looking Forward

So, as we close this chapter, what does the future hold for Gen Alpha? It's almost impossible to predict. The world they're inheriting is complex, full of potential yet shadowed by uncertainties. They have choices, and they have the tools to make them, but the path they'll take remains unwritten. Perhaps, in the end, it will be Gen Alpha's willingness to embrace the unknown, their readiness to adapt, and their drive to personalize their journeys that will define their legacy.

Only time will tell. And maybe, for Gen Alpha, that's just how they like it.

Appendix A: College Financial Planning Terms

Presented here is a list of thirty important terms to understand relating to college financial planning along with their definitions:

Expected Family Contribution (EFC): The amount a family is expected to contribute toward a student's college expenses, determined by the FAFSA (Free Application for Federal Student Aid).

Financial Aid: Funds provided to students to help cover the cost of their education, including grants, scholarships, loans, and work-study programs.

Grants: Financial aid that does not need to be repaid and is typically based on financial need.

Scholarships: Funds awarded to students based on academic, athletic, or other achievements. Scholarships do not require repayment.

Work-Study: A federal program that provides part-time jobs for students to help them earn money to cover educational expenses.

Cost of Attendance (COA): The total cost of attending college, including tuition, fees, room and board, books, and other expenses.

Net Price: The amount a student pays for college after subtracting grants and scholarships from the total cost.

Tuition: The cost of the academic courses and instruction at a college or university.

Room and Board: The cost of on-campus or off-campus housing and meals.

Federal Student Aid (FSA): Financial assistance provided by the U.S. Department of Education to help students pay for college.

Federal Pell Grant: A need-based federal grant awarded to undergraduate students to help cover educational expenses.

Federal Direct Subsidized Loan: A federal student loan based on financial need, with interest payments subsidized by the government while the student is in school.

Federal Direct Unsubsidized Loan: A federal student loan not based on financial need, with interest accruing while the student is in school.

Federal PLUS Loan: A federal loan available to parents of dependent undergraduate students or graduate students, covering educational expenses.

Free Application for Federal Student Aid (FAFSA): A form used to apply for federal and state financial aid programs, including grants, loans, and work-study.

Merit-Based Aid: Financial assistance, such as scholarships, awarded based on academic, athletic, or other achievements, rather than financial need.

Financial Aid Package: The total combination of financial aid (grants, scholarships, loans, and work-study) offered to a student.

Loan Forgiveness: The cancellation of student loan debt under specific conditions, such as public service or income-driven repayment.

Deferment: A period during which a borrower can temporarily postpone student loan payments, typically due to enrollment in school or economic hardship.

Default: Failure to repay a student loan according to the terms of the promissory note, resulting in serious consequences, including legal action and damaged credit.

In-School Interest: Interest that accrues on student loans while the borrower is still in school or during deferment.

Interest Rate: The cost of borrowing money, typically expressed as an annual percentage rate (APR).

Grace Period: A set period (usually six months) after graduation or leaving school during which student loan borrowers are not required to make payments.

529 Plan: A tax-advantaged savings plan designed to encourage saving for future college expenses.

Parental Contribution: The amount parents are expected to contribute to their child's education, often assessed during financial aid evaluations.

Cost-Benefit Analysis: An evaluation of the potential financial returns compared to the costs associated with pursuing a college degree.

Financial Literacy: The knowledge and skills needed to make informed financial decisions, including managing college expenses.

Community College: A two-year institution that offers lower-cost general education courses and an opportunity to transfer to a four-year college or university.

College ROI (Return on Investment): The financial benefits of obtaining a college degree compared to the costs incurred.

Loan Consolidation: The process of combining multiple student loans into a single loan, often with extended repayment terms or lower monthly payments.

Appendix B: Financial Quiz

Open book, open notes. No time limit.

[some questions have multiple correct answers]

You have completed reading the book and the previous appendix on College Financial Planning Terms. You are now ready for our short quiz. Good luck.

Here's a quiz with ten critical questions aimed at high school and college students in the United States who aspire to obtain a college degree with ZERO PERSONAL DEBT upon graduation. These questions cover essential issues and knowledge areas that can help them work towards these challenging goals:

1. Question: What is the Free Application for Federal Student Aid (FAFSA), and why is it necessary for college financial planning?

A. A scholarship application

B. A student loan application

C. A federal financial aid application

D. A college admission application

2. Question: True or False: Scholarships and grants do not need to be repaid, making them valuable sources of financial aid for college.

3. Question: Which of the following is a critical factor in determining your Expected Family Contribution (EFC) for federal financial aid purposes?

A. Family income and assets

B. Student's GPA

C. Choice of major

D. SAT/ACT scores

4. Question: What is the significance of the "net price" of a college?

A. The total cost of attendance

B. The cost of tuition only

C. The amount you'll pay after grants and scholarships

D. The price of textbooks and supplies

5. Question: Which strategies can help minimize college costs? (Select all that apply)

A. Taking Advanced Placement (AP) courses in high school

B. Attending a community college before transferring to a four-year institution

C. Living off-campus instead of in a dormitory

D. Taking out the maximum amount of student loans available

6. Question: What does "work-study" refer to in the context of college financial aid?

A. A scholarship for working students

B. Federal grants for low-income students

C. A part-time job program that helps students earn money to pay for education

D. A student loan program with deferred interest

7. Question: True or False: It's a sound financial strategy to pay for college tuition using a high-interest credit card.

8. Question: What is the role of a financial advisor or counselor in college financial planning?

A. To provide guidance on which college to attend

B. To help students select their major

C. To offer financial planning advice and assist in finding scholarships and grants

D. To help students complete their homework assignments

9. Question: Which factors can impact the total cost of obtaining a college degree?

A. The length of time it takes to graduate

B. The number of student loans you take out

C. Your choice of major

D. The type of housing you select

10. Question: What does "financial literacy" mean when managing college finances, and why is it important for students?

A. The ability to count money accurately

B. The knowledge and skills to make informed financial decisions and manage money effectively

C. The act of saving all income and not spending it

D. The process of investing in stocks and bonds

Answers:

1. C

2. True

3. A

4. C

5. A, B

6. C

7. False

8. C

9. A, B, C, D

10. B

Appendix C: The Common App

Here's a comprehensive checklist for high school students to complete the Common Application (@CommonApp). This list is designed to keep you organized and ensure you don't miss any key steps in the process.

1. Create Your Common App Account

- Visit CommonApp.org and create an account.

- Set up your profile with personal details like name, email, and contact information.

2. Research Colleges

- Use the college search tool to find schools that interest you.

- Add schools to your "My Colleges" list.

- Research application requirements for each school (deadlines, essays, standardized tests, etc.).

3. Personal Information

- Complete the "Profile" section with your basic personal details, including:

- Full name, gender, birthdate, and citizenship status.

- Contact information (address, phone number).

- Demographic information.

- Family details (parent/guardian information).

4. Educational Information

- Fill in the "Education" section with:

- Current high school name and details.

- Academic honors and recognitions.

- Courses and grades (especially if required by your selected schools).

- Senior year schedule (classes you're taking).

- College courses (if applicable).

5. Standardized Testing

- Input test scores (SAT, ACT, AP, IB) in the "Testing" section.

- Ensure schools require/recommend scores before submitting.

- Send official test scores directly through testing agencies (College Board/ACT).

6. Activities

- Fill out the "Activities" section to showcase extracurricular involvement (clubs, sports, jobs, volunteering).

- You can list up to 10 activities.

- Prioritize leadership roles, commitment, and relevance to your goals.

- Include a brief description for each activity.

7. Writing (Essays)

- Personal Statement: Write and upload your Common App essay (250–650 words).

- Respond to one of the Common App essay prompts.

- Edit and proofread carefully.

- Supplemental Essays: Check if your chosen schools require additional essays.

- Review and draft answers for each school's specific prompts.

- Proofread and seek feedback from teachers or mentors.

8. Letters of Recommendation

- Request recommendation letters from teachers, counselors, or other recommenders.

- Make requests well in advance (4-6 weeks before the deadline).

- Assign recommenders through the "Recommenders and FERPA" section.

- Complete the FERPA Waiver to waive your right to view recommendations (this is often recommended to ensure honest feedback).

9. Counselor Information

- Ensure your counselor submits your School Report and Transcript.

- Speak with your counselor early to confirm submission deadlines.

- Follow up to ensure that documents are sent.

10. Review Application

- Review each section for accuracy and completeness.

- Double-check spelling, grammar, and information consistency.

- Ensure all sections are complete before submission.

11. Pay Application Fees

- Submit your application fees (or request a fee waiver if eligible).

- Check each college's fee policy.

- Complete the Common App Fee Waiver section if you qualify.

12. Submit Your Application

- Submit each application individually through the Common App.

- Make sure all sections (essays, activities, test scores, recommendations, etc.) are submitted.

- Confirm submission by receiving confirmation emails from Common App and the colleges.

13. Follow Up

- Track your application status through the Common App and each school's portal.

- Follow up on missing documents (transcripts, recommendations) as needed.

- Keep an eye on email for application updates, interviews, and additional requests from colleges.

Pro Tips

Start Early: Avoid last-minute stress by starting the application process well in advance.

Stay Organized: Use a calendar or spreadsheet to track application deadlines and requirements.

Seek Feedback: Have a teacher, counselor, or trusted adult review your essays and application.

Be Yourself: Show your authentic self in your writing and activity descriptions.

This checklist will help guide you through each stage of the Common App process and ensure you submit your best possible application.

Appendix D: Top 10 Cities for Gen Z

The following U.S. cities have been ranked in the top 10 according to the percentage of Gen Z occupants. Yes, all of these cities have a strong college presence associated with these locations.

1. Ann Arbor, Michigan

2. Provo, Utah

3. Boulder, Colorado

4. College Station, Texas

5. Athens, Georgia

6. Tallahassee, Florida

7. Berkeley, California

8. Gainesville, Florida

9. Columbia, South Carolina

10. Syracuse, New York

sources: U.S. Census Bureau, 2022; SmartAsset

States Raining Cash

Financial Incentives to Move

Five states are offering up to $20,000 for new residents to call their new home.

West Virginia, Kansas, Oklahoma, Indiana and Kentucky are among the prime states offering real financial incentives to welcome new residents

The offers range from $5,000 in Indiana and Kentucky to $20,000 in West Virginia

States with ZERO State Income Tax

"Live Free or Die" is the official motto of the U.S. state of New Hampshire, adopted by the state in 1945.

The following states boast no state income tax.

Texas

Alaska

Florida

Wyoming

Nevada

Tennessee

Washington

South Dakota

New Hampshire

source: Tax Foundation, 2024.

Appendix E: Merit Based Scholarships

Merit-based scholarships are financial awards given to students based on their academic, artistic, athletic, or other achievements, rather than financial need. These scholarships are designed to reward students for their hard work and accomplishments. They can come from colleges, private organizations, corporations, or non-profits. Requirements usually include high GPA, standardized test scores, leadership roles, extracurricular activities, and sometimes an essay or interview process. They significantly help reduce the cost of tuition, making higher education more accessible for high-achieving students.

This is a brief list of select scholarships awarded by certain universities along with additional merit-based scholarship opportunities that U.S. students should consider.

Jefferson Scholars Program (University of Virginia)

This highly competitive merit-based scholarship aims to cover the full cost of attendance at the University of Virginia. It rewards students who demonstrate exceptional leadership, scholarship, and citizenship. Jefferson Scholars participate in enrichment programs and receive mentorship to foster their growth throughout their college journey. This program is for full-time enrollment across eight semesters at the University of Virginia.

Trustee Scholarship (Boston University)

Boston University's Trustee Scholarship is a full-tuition merit scholarship for undergraduate students with outstanding academic records and leadership potential. Scholars join a special honors community and benefit from personalized advising and academic enrichment opportunities.

Robertson Scholars Leadership Program (Duke and UNC-Chapel Hill)

This unique scholarship is offered jointly by Duke University and the University of North Carolina at Chapel Hill. Robertson Scholars receive full tuition, room, and board, along with summer funding for leadership development opportunities. It seeks to cultivate future leaders by combining resources from both universities.

Cornelius Vanderbilt Scholarship (Vanderbilt University)

This merit-based scholarship covers full tuition at Vanderbilt and is awarded to students who demonstrate exceptional leadership and intellectual achievement. In addition to the financial award, Cornelius Vanderbilt Scholars benefit from unique academic and leadership enrichment activities.

Additional Merit-Based Scholarship Opportunities:

Stamps Scholars Program

The Stamps Scholarship is a prestigious merit-based program available at many U.S. universities. It provides full tuition, room, board, and enrichment funds to top students. Stamps Scholars are selected for their academic excellence, leadership skills, and perseverance.

The Coolidge Scholarship

This national scholarship is awarded to students who demonstrate outstanding academic achievement, a deep interest in public policy, and leadership potential. It covers the full cost of tuition, room, board, and expenses for undergraduate studies. The Coolidge scholarship can be applied to any accredited college or university in the U.S.

The Coca-Cola Scholarship

The Coca-Cola Scholars Program provides merit-based scholarships to students who exemplify leadership and service. It awards $20,000 to high school seniors who have made a significant impact on their schools and communities (150 students are chosen as Coca-Cola Scholars annually).

Elks Most Valuable Student Scholarship

The Elks National Foundation awards scholarships to students based on leadership, academic achievement, and financial need. Top recipients may receive up to $50,000 in scholarship money, and finalists attend a national leadership weekend. The Elks awards 500 four-year scholarships to top applicants in the 2025 competition.

Gates Scholarship

Funded by the Bill & Melinda Gates Foundation, this highly selective scholarship supports high-achieving minority students. It covers the full cost of attendance not already covered by other financial aid sources.

Jack Kent Cooke Foundation Scholarship

This scholarship provides up to $55,000 annually to high-performing students with financial need. The foundation supports students from high school through graduate school, offering both financial aid and academic support.

National Merit Scholarship

High school students who perform exceptionally well on the PSAT/NMSQT are eligible for National Merit Scholarships. These awards are based on academic achievement, recommendations, and extracurricular involvement.

Davidson Fellows Scholarship

The Davidson Institute for Talent Development offers scholarships of $50,000, $25,000, and $10,000 to gifted students who have completed significant projects in areas like science, technology, engineering, math, literature, and music.

U.S. Presidential Scholars Program

This prestigious program recognizes up to 161 students each year for outstanding academic achievement, artistic excellence, leadership, and community involvement. While it does not offer a financial award, it is one of the highest honors for graduating seniors.

These scholarships reward academic excellence, leadership, and extracurricular achievements. Many offer full financial coverage, leadership development, and networking opportunities, making them highly competitive but incredibly valuable for students.

Appendix F: Common App Direct Admissions

Common App Direct Admissions is a proactive admissions process designed to simplify and streamline the path to college for students. This is how it works and the benefits it offers:

How It Works

Eligibility: Participating colleges (117 schools) set specific requirements, such as a minimum GPA. Common App identifies students who meet these criteria based on the information in their Common App profiles.

Notification: Students who qualify receive direct admissions offers in their Common App accounts and via email. These offers are non-binding, meaning students are not obligated to enroll if they choose to apply.

Application: If a student decides to apply using the direct admissions offer, they can do so without paying an application fee. The college will then review the application to ensure it meets all criteria, including any specific program or major requirements.

Benefits for Students

Reduced Stress: Knowing they have a college offer can significantly reduce the stress and uncertainty associated with the college application process.

Cost Savings: Students save on application fees, which can add up when applying to multiple colleges.

Confidence Boost: Receiving an offer based on their existing profile can boost students' confidence and motivation1.

Informed Decisions: Students have the opportunity to learn more about the colleges that have extended offers, helping them make more informed decisions about where to apply and enroll.

Overall, Common App Direct Admissions aims to make the college admissions process more accessible and less daunting, especially for first-generation and low- to middle-income students.

The participating colleges and universities in the program come from 35 states.

Alabama

Auburn University at Montgomery

Alaska

University of Alaska Fairbanks

Arkansas

Hendrix College

California

Menlo College

Mount Saint Mary's University Los Angeles

Saint Mary's College of California

University of the Pacific

Whittier College

Colorado

Metropolitan State University of Denver (MSU Denver)

Naropa University

Regis University

Florida

Eckerd College

Saint Leo University

Stetson University

Georgia

Brenau University

Georgia State University

Oglethorpe University

Illinois

Columbia College Chicago

Elmhurst University

Illinois Institute of Technology

Illinois Wesleyan University

Millikin University

Monmouth College (IL)

Indiana

University of Evansville

University of Saint Francis

Wabash College

Iowa

St. Ambrose University

Kansas

Kansas State University

Kentucky

Spalding University

Thomas More University

Transylvania University

University of Kentucky

Maryland

Coppin State University

Towson University

Washington College

University of Maryland Eastern Shore

Massachusetts

Fisher College

Hampshire College

Lasell University

Merrimack College

Regis College

Salem State University

University of Massachusetts Boston

University of Massachusetts Lowell

Western New England University

Westfield State University

Michigan

Central Michigan University

Madonna University

Minnesota

Augsburg University

College of St. Benedict

Concordia University, St. Paul

Hamline University (MN)

Saint John's University (MN)

The College of St. Scholastica

Missouri

Maryville University of St. Louis

Truman State University

Nebraska

Nebraska Wesleyan University

New Hampshire

Keene State College

New Jersey

Centenary University

Felician University

Kean University

Rider University

Saint Elizabeth University

Stockton University

Nevada

University of Nevada, Reno

New York

Iona University

Manhattan College

Manhattanville University

Mercy University

Nazareth University

New York Institute of Technology (NYIT)

Niagara University

Paul Smith's College

St. Thomas Aquinas College

SUNY Buffalo State University

The New School

Wagner College

North Carolina

Methodist University

University of North Carolina Asheville

Wingate University

Ohio

College of Wooster

Hiram College

Wittenberg University

Oklahoma

Oral Roberts University

Oregon

Oregon Tech

Portland State University

Pennsylvania

Allegheny College

Arcadia University

Chatham Universit

Immaculata University

King's College

Lincoln University (PA)

Moravian University

Neumann University

Pennsylvania Western University

Robert Morris University (PA)

Rosemont College

York College of Pennsylvania

Rhode Island

Salve Regina University

South Carolina

Spartanburg Methodist College

Tennessee

The University of Memphis

Texas

Austin College

Houston Christian University

McMurry University

Southern Methodist University

St. Edward's University

University of Texas Arlington

Virginia

Christopher Newport University

Emory & Henry University

George Mason University

Marymount University

Richard Bland College of William and Mary

University of Lynchburg

Virginia Commonwealth University

Vermont

Vermont State University

Washington

Whitworth University

Wisconsin

St. Norbert College

Appendix G: Saving Money on Textbooks

For undergraduate students looking to cut costs, managing the high expense of textbooks is a major area where savings can be realized. The key is to move away from costly campus bookstores and explore cheaper or even free alternatives. One student's experience at Vanderbilt shows that while the convenience of the campus bookstore is tempting, it is often the most expensive option. Fortunately, there are many more affordable and accessible resources to consider, all of which can help save money each semester.

Tips for Cost Savings:

1. Online Marketplaces: Websites like AbeBooks, BooksRun, and Chegg offer students the chance to purchase or rent textbooks at far lower prices than university bookstores. With options to buy used books, students can save a significant amount by opting for cheaper second-hand versions, many of which still have years of life left in them. Additionally, services like Chegg provide free shipping on rentals and free returns, making it both affordable and convenient for students on a budget.

2. Price Comparison: Platforms such as Biblio aggregate prices from various sellers, allowing students to compare offers and select the most cost-effective option. Price comparison ensures students avoid paying more than necessary while still getting the exact textbooks they need.

3. Selling or Trading Books: One highly underrated strategy is buying and selling textbooks among fellow students. At the end of the semester, rather than letting books collect dust, students can sell or trade them. BooksRun even offers an option for students to sell their textbooks back. Additionally, bartering directly with other students on campus — through social media groups, student forums, or even informal book swaps — can be a way to avoid spending any money at all.

4. Sharing and Bartering: Don't underestimate the power of community on campus. Borrowing or trading books with friends, roommates, or classmates is an excellent way to avoid spending money altogether. Many students often take the same core courses, making book swaps practical. For example, a psychology major might trade their general chemistry book for a peer's psychology textbook, cutting down costs without sacrificing access to essential learning materials.

Conclusion:

By utilizing these cost-saving strategies — from buying used books online to swapping with friends — undergraduates can dramatically reduce their textbook expenses. Avoiding the campus bookstore except as a last resort, exploring cheaper online platforms, and trading within their campus community are excellent ways to keep more money in their pockets while still getting the materials they need.

Appendix H: Hacker House

Why Tech College Students Should Join or Form a Hacker House to Lead the AI Revolution

In the fast-evolving world of AI, tech students have a unique opportunity to be at the forefront of innovation, and one of the most effective ways to do this is by joining or forming a hacker house. Hacker houses are collaborative living spaces where like-minded individuals, students, tech enthusiasts, and entrepreneurs live and work together on cutting-edge projects. Here's why every tech student should consider this path to accelerate their involvement in the AI race:

1. Collaborative Innovation

Hacker houses foster a unique, highly collaborative environment where the brightest minds can come together. Residents share ideas, skills, and resources, creating a synergistic atmosphere for innovation. This is crucial in AI, where breakthroughs often come from cross-disciplinary thinking. By surrounding yourself with other ambitious tech enthusiasts, you'll not only stay ahead of trends but also have the chance to co-create solutions that can change industries.

2. Cost-Effective Learning and Experimentation

AI research and development can be expensive, and many students face financial constraints. Hacker houses offer a cost-effective living solution by sharing rent, utilities, and resources. This setup allows residents to focus more on experimenting with AI projects and less on financial burdens. This is essential for students who want to prototype ideas and build portfolio-worthy projects. Some houses are able to secure funding from investors.

3. Access to Networking Opportunities

Living in a hacker house provides unparalleled networking opportunities. You'll be living with other tech-savvy individuals, many of whom might become co-founders, collaborators, or even the next AI pioneers. In addition to daily interactions, hacker houses often attract attention from investors, startup mentors, and venture capitalists. The connections made in such an environment can be the difference between a project staying in the lab and becoming the next breakthrough technology.

4. A Supportive Ecosystem for AI Ambitions

Hacker houses naturally build a support network where residents motivate each other, exchange knowledge, and tackle challenges together. This supportive atmosphere is especially beneficial in AI, where learning curves are steep, and setbacks are frequent. Whether you need help debugging an AI model, guidance on research papers, or advice on securing funding, there's always someone nearby to lend support.

5. Proximity to Tech Hubs

Many hacker houses are situated in tech-centric areas like San Francisco, New York, and Silicon Valley, where AI and machine learning innovation thrive. Being in proximity to these tech hubs gives you access to AI conferences, workshops, and other events, all while living in a space that enhances your productivity and creativity.

6. Real-World AI Experience

Beyond networking and collaboration, hacker houses give residents the chance to work on real-world projects that could have significant impacts. From building AI-driven startups to collaborating on open-source AI tools, the projects born in hacker houses are often practical, hands-on, and directly tied to the tech industry's needs.

7. Empowerment to Lead in AI

Perhaps most importantly, forming or joining a hacker house empowers you to lead in AI. You are surrounded by individuals who share your vision and passion for technology, giving you the platform to explore innovative ideas without the constraints of a traditional classroom. In a hacker house, you're not just learning AI; you're actively participating in creating its future.

Conclusion

For tech college students aiming to join the AI revolution, there's no better place to start than a hacker house. These unique living spaces offer an unparalleled combination of collaboration, financial feasibility, networking, and support—all of which are essential ingredients for leading in the world of AI. By joining or forming a hacker house, you position yourself not just as a participant in the AI race but as a leader, capable of transforming ideas into world-changing innovations.

Hacker House Funding

Hacker houses can indeed seek funding from a variety of sources, including angel investors and venture capital, depending on the goals and projects pursued within the house. Here's a breakdown of funding options and known sources that hacker houses can tap into:

1. Angel Investors

Angel investors are often individuals who provide early-stage funding to startups or tech ventures, and they could be interested in funding hacker houses, especially if they see potential in the projects coming out of these spaces. Hacker houses often house innovative startups or high-potential projects, which could appeal to angel investors looking for cutting-edge tech opportunities. Some angel investors may even prefer to invest in the hacker house concept as a hub for nurturing multiple ideas, rather than funding just one startup.

2. Venture Capital

Venture capital (VC) firms generally provide funding to startups that are further along in their development, but some VC firms might invest in hacker houses, especially if they see them as innovation hubs that can churn out multiple viable startups. Venture capitalists might be more interested if the hacker house is associated with tech startups or AI ventures with high growth potential. For example, houses that produce innovative AI-driven startups might attract attention from VCs specializing in artificial intelligence and deep tech.

3. Grants and Startup Competitions

Another potential source of funding is through innovation grants or startup competitions. Some universities, tech incubators, and government initiatives offer grants to spaces fostering innovation, which includes hacker houses. For example, AI and tech-focused competitions often provide grants or seed money that hacker house projects could qualify for. Popular competitions like TechCrunch Disrupt, MIT 100K, or YC Startup School can provide exposure and potential funding.

4. Corporate Partnerships

Tech companies often look to collaborate with hacker houses as they serve as experimental hubs for cutting-edge tech. For instance, large corporations like Google, Microsoft, or NVIDIA have been known to offer support through grants, sponsorships, or resource-sharing for hacker houses working on projects in fields like AI, blockchain, or cloud computing. This not only gives hacker houses funding but also access to crucial resources and mentorship.

5. Crowdfunding Platforms

Platforms like Kickstarter, GoFundMe, or Indiegogo allow hacker houses to raise funds directly from the public. If the house focuses on an exciting, forward-thinking project that resonates with a wider audience, crowdfunding can provide the necessary capital while also promoting the house and its work.

6. Accelerator Programs

Some hacker houses might consider joining an accelerator program. While not direct funding for the house itself, many tech accelerators like Y Combinator, 500 Startups, and Techstars offer seed funding, mentorship, and resources for startup ideas that could be coming out of a hacker house. If the house produces a startup ready for acceleration, this could be a great route for receiving structured funding.

7. Real Estate Investors

Since hacker houses are both living and working spaces, real estate investors interested in co-living or co-working spaces could also provide funding. If the hacker house is located in a high-demand tech hub (such as Silicon Valley or New York), real estate investors may see the property as a lucrative venture in itself and be willing to fund or partner with the house as an investment in future startups.

8. University and Research Funding

Many university-affiliated hacker houses or tech projects receive backing from educational institutions. Research grants or tech innovation funds from universities can support hacker houses, especially those focusing on AI, machine learning, or robotics. If the house is composed of tech students or graduates, universities may see it as an extension of their innovation initiatives.

Examples of Hacker House Funding

Hack VC: A venture capital fund with a specific focus on supporting hacker houses and tech talent across various sectors.

On Deck Fellowship: While primarily a talent accelerator, it has supported hacker house-like communities and projects through its network.

GitHub Grants: GitHub has been known to offer grants or support to open-source projects, some of which have emerged from hacker houses.

In summary, hacker houses can seek funding from angel investors, venture capitalists, corporate partnerships, crowdfunding, real estate investors, and even through grants or accelerator programs. The key is to align the house's mission and the potential of its residents' projects with the right type of investor or funding body.

Appendix I: Get a U.S. Passport

If you want to become a Digital Nomad, you'll need a passport, of course, to begin your global journey.

You'll also need a passport if you attend college and join a study abroad program. An international program can become an integral part of an undergraduate's college career.

Regardless of how you employ your passport, it is also wise to obtain it sooner than wait until the last moment when you would need to rush to obtain one.

Basic Steps to Secure a U.S. Passport

Securing a U.S. passport involves several steps. Here's a breakdown of the process, including how to expedite it.

- Complete the Application Form:

- For first-time applicants, fill out Form DS-11.

- For renewals, use Form DS-82.

- Gather Required Documents:

- Proof of U.S. citizenship (e.g., birth certificate, naturalization certificate).

- Government-issued photo ID (e.g., driver's license).

- Photocopies of both documents.

- Get a Passport Photo:

- Ensure it meets the specific requirements (2x2 inches, color, taken within the last six months).

- Pay the Fees:

- Standard fees include the application fee and the execution fee.

- Fees vary depending on the type of passport and processing speed.

- Submit Your Application:

- First-time applicants must apply in person at a passport acceptance facility.

- Renewals can often be done by mail.

- Wait for Processing:

- Standard processing time is typically 6-8 weeks.

- Expedited Passport Steps- Request Expedited Service:

- Indicate on your application that you need expedited processing.

- Pay the additional expedited fee.

- Submit Your Application:

- You can apply in person at a passport acceptance facility or a regional passport agency.

- For urgent travel (within 14 days), make an appointment at a regional passport agency.

- Processing Time:

- Expedited processing typically takes 3-4 weeks.

For more detailed information, you can visit the U.S. Department of State's passport website.

https://travel.state.gov

9 798227 656940